Sharon Whittaker

ELEMENTARY

Total English

DIGITAL
User's Guide

PEARSON
Longman

PROMETHEAN

Contents

Introduction

Total English Digital is the interactive whiteboard software for use with *Total English* course books. We recognise that learning to use interactive whiteboards, like any new piece of technology, can be intimidating, so this guide aims to give you a jargon-free introduction to using interactive whiteboards in your classroom. The software has been designed to use the reliable content taken from the *Total English Students' Book* in an interactive way that increases student motivation and saves you time.

What is an interactive whiteboard, and how does it work with *Total English Digital*?

An interactive whiteboard is a piece of hardware that looks much like a standard whiteboard, but it connects to a computer and a projector in the classroom to make a very powerful tool. When connected, the interactive whiteboard becomes a giant, touch-sensitive version of the computer screen. Instead of using the mouse, you can control your computer through the interactive whiteboard screen just by touching it with a special pen (or, on some types of boards, with your finger). Anything that can be accessed from your computer can be accessed and displayed on the interactive whiteboard, for example Word documents, PowerPoint presentations, photographs, websites or online materials.

Using special software included with the interactive whiteboard, you can also interact with images and text projected on the board: rearranging them, changing their size, colour, etc. This offers a much more interactive experience than using a standard whiteboard or using a data projector alone.

Total English Digital and this guide provide an excellent starting point in building your confidence with the interactive whiteboard and teaching you about the tools you need and how to use them. The *Total English Digital* software follows the same layout with the same contents as the coursebook. This makes it immediately recognisable and quick and easy to switch between using the book and the interactive whiteboard in class.

What are the benefits of interactive whiteboards and *Total English Digital*?

When you use *Total English Digital*, it will help you understand the benefits of interactive whiteboards in the language classroom.

Convenient and time-saving

Total English Digital acts as a 'one-stop-shop' for all of the *Total English* resources. The Students' Book, listening files, tapescripts and videos as well as selected interactive flipcharts (activities specially-prepared for use on an interactive whiteboard using special software called Activstudio) are all easily accessible in one place and displayed on the interactive whiteboard.

Just by touching the interactive whiteboard screen, you can move quickly and easily from an activity in the Students' Book to an audio track, perhaps looking at the tapescript for post-listening work before returning to the Students' Book. This helps you adapt the pace of your lesson according to the needs of the group and saves lots of time. No more cueing CDs or DVDs!

Focuses students' attention

The interactive whiteboard provides a useful focal point in the class. Instead of asking learners to focus on a picture or instruction in the book, you can zoom into the relevant section of the page and magnify it many times on the interactive whiteboard. Just click on any part of the page to make it zoom.

The clear icons and simple controls mean that you and your students can work directly with the interactive whiteboard and avoid going back and forth from the computer to the board. Because you can stay at the front of the classroom, it is easier to keep students' attention focused on the activity at hand.

Engages different types of learners

Some students prefer to listen and absorb, others respond well to pictures, while others respond well to physical interaction. *Total English Digital* supports users with all these preferences through its rich multi-media, audio-visual and flipchart content. The flipcharts involve a range of simple interactions, such as drag and drop, erase or write-in.

The simplicity of these exercise types means that your learners can interact with the materials with no previous typing or IT skills, facilitating more student-centred lessons. Learning becomes more active and, therefore, more memorable.

Helpful and supportive

This guide includes teacher's notes for every flipchart with suggestions on how to teach the lesson using the interactive whiteboard. There are also teaching tips and suggestions on how to exploit the flipcharts and materials further.

By using *Total English Digital*, you'll become familiar with interactive whiteboard technology in general and develop a repertoire of approaches to suit your teaching style. Gradually, *Total English Digital* will give you the confidence to create your own flipchart activities.

Adds variety

Total English Digital is an additional way of presenting *Total English* coursebook material in your lesson. It is not, however, designed to replace the book for the student, nor is it designed to dominate your classroom teaching throughout each lesson. In any classroom situation it is important to select the appropriate tool, approach or materials to best achieve your teaching objectives.

You may, for example, only want to use *Total English Digital* to introduce an activity to be completed in the book or to conduct feedback after a pair or group activity.

How do I teach with *Total English Digital*?

Total English Digital cuts down on preparation time and aims to make teaching with an interactive whiteboard easy. As with any tool, the more familiar you are with it, the easier you will find it and the more confident you will feel in class. In the initial stages, you might prefer to limit your use of the software in class to the 'zoomable' page spreads and the easy-access audio, tapescripts and videos. When you are comfortable with these, you can move on to use the flipcharts.

Familiarise yourself

If you can, look at all the interactive materials available in *Total English Digital*, including the flipchart activities, audio and tapescripts for the module you are about to teach. Not all of the parts of the page have flipcharts but all parts of the book can be magnified to draw students' focus. Think about how and when the interactive whiteboard will make an impact in your lesson. When is it best to use interactive activities, and when is it best for students to work in their books?

Think about how students will be interacting at different stages of the lesson, in whole class, small groups or individual learning mode. At what stages will the learners be actively using the board, and at what stages will it be providing visual support? And don't forget to give your students a break from the digital edition! Sometimes switching the board off/muting the projector can be less distracting and help students focus better on the task in hand, especially with small group and discussion tasks. Remember to think about variety and balance.

Familiarise yourself with the mechanics of each digital activity and check if it requires drag and drop, erase or write-in. A small tool icon in the rubric reminds you which tool to use. Even though you'll be encouraging your students to do the hands-on work at the board, you'll need to provide both language and technical support on occasions.

Before the class, it's a good idea to check the flipchart and see where the answers appear on the page. In the interests of legibility, this will help you direct your students to write their answers in an appropriate place. The step-by-step unit notes in this guide will help you with this.

Manage the classroom

The interactive whiteboard offers great opportunities for student-centred work at the board, but classroom management is crucial. With gap-fill type activities, for example, it can be time-consuming getting different students out to the board for each answer and can slow the pace of your lesson. Resist the temptation to take over the board yourself but rather experiment with ways that work for your group. Depending on the activity type, you might nominate a 'board assistant' for one activity. S/he could elicit answers from the class. Or perhaps use an 'early finisher' or invite individual students to come out while an activity is in progress. In this way the book and interactive whiteboard versions are completed at the same time and the interactive whiteboard provides ongoing feedback.

Reading

With reading activities it is generally more appropriate for students to read the text in their books. The interactive whiteboard provides an excellent focus for pre-reading work and also for post-reading text analysis: highlighting features of the text or vocabulary is a very effective use of the interactive whiteboard.

Writing

If you are preparing students for a writing task, images from the unit make good prompts for brainstorming content and ideas. You might decide to use model texts from the book for process writing activities and can, for example, ask your students to highlight certain features of the text in different colours.

Speaking

In the same way, when planning speaking you may plan to exploit the on-screen tapescripts as model dialogues, highlighting features of spoken discourse in preparation for the main speaking task in the module. You may wish to zoom in on instructions and draw students' attention to key words to make sure they understand what they have to do. You may decide to leave these instructions on screen as they work, or alternatively, zoom in on the *How To …* boxes sections to support the students in their task. As part of general classroom practice, you might drill phrases from these sections, pointing out stress or intonation patterns, so that learners are using a correct model.

Consider if or when you will show the tapescript, and what you will do with it. Decide if there are any useful phrases you want to bring to your students' attention and highlight these with one of the writing tools.

Pronunciation

Pronunciation activities can often be more effective if students are concentrating on imitating the sounds they hear and not trying to read at the same time. This is a good opportunity to ask students to close their books and try to imitate your model or the audio file in *Total English Digital*. You can use the interactive whiteboard to annotate features you want to focus on, for example, stress patterns or phonemic symbols then cover up the patterns so the students practise without reading.

Grammar

In Grammar activities, read through the instructions in the flipchart to see if there are key words you need to explain. You can use the writing tools to highlight these on the board to make sure all your students understand what is expected of them.

Zoom in on the Active grammar boxes or the Reference pages. Use them to teach difficult grammar ideas and give contextualised examples to further support your learners.

Vocabulary

Look at the amount and level of vocabulary coming up in your lesson and decide at what stages of the lesson and how you will introduce it. You can pre-teach phrases by zooming in on pictures from the unit or bringing in other digital images.

Consider how and where you will record new words that come up. You may wish to record them on a blank flipchart or Word document.

Use other resources

You may want to use other traditional or digital resources, for example, a web page, online dictionaries or other teaching materials. Check that any content to be shown on the interactive whiteboard will be visible from the back of the classroom. Try to have digital resources minimised before the lesson so you don't have to search through folders or links during lesson time.

Does the type of interactive whiteboard I'm using make a difference?

No matter what kind of interactive whiteboard you are using, the basic way to use the program is the same.

Promethean interactive whiteboards

If you are using a Promethean interactive whiteboard, *Total English Digital* will launch the 'Professional Edition' of Activstudio software that came with the whiteboard. This version of the software is slightly different from the software described in this guide. You may notice these differences:

- The toolbar is likely to have more tools than the one shown in this guide, but you can use the tools shown in this guide in the same way.
- You are able to have up to five flipcharts open at the same time, including a blank flipchart for note-taking or brainstorming. Any flipchart you create from scratch can be saved.
- You can write/highlight on top of the page spreads when they are zoomed or not zoomed by using 'Annotate-over-desktop' functionality.
- You can use other tools such as a timer, an on-screen keyboard, a link to the internet, etc

Contact your Promethean hardware provider for advice on how to use these additional functions.

Smart, Hitachi Starboard, Ebeam, Polyvision, Mimio or other interactive whiteboards

If you are using a different type of interactive whiteboard, the basic way to use the program remains the same because of the special Activstudio software that is installed as part of *Total English Digital*. By using the software that comes with your interactive whiteboard as well as the tools shown in this guide, you can:

- Write/highlight on top of the page spreads when they are zoomed or not zoomed.
- Have a blank flipchart open for note-taking or brainstorming. These flipcharts can be saved.
- Use other tools such as a timer, an on-screen keyboard, a link to the internet, etc.

Contact your hardware provider for advice on how to use these additional functions.

Support

Pearson Longman wants to help you to feel confident when teaching from *Total English Digital*. If you experience difficulties while using the software, follow these steps until the problem is resolved:

1. Consult the FAQ in this guide (page 11).
2. Restart your computer.
3. Turn the projector and interactive whiteboard off and then on again.
4. Consult the manual that accompanies your interactive whiteboard.
5. If you think it is a problem with your interactive whiteboard, contact the hardware provider.
6. If you think it is a problem with *Total English Digital*, please email the Pearson Longman technical support team at elt-support@pearson.com.

Comments/feedback

Pearson Longman strives to produce high quality products that meet your teaching needs. Please send your comments/feedback about the product to digitaldelivery@pearson.com.

Get started

Total English Digital home page

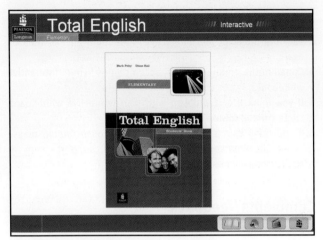

Total English Digital is divided into four sections which are accessible through buttons on the home page you see when you install or run the program:

You can move to another section by clicking on the icons:

 Students' Book section to view pages and select interactive whiteboard activities

 Go to Audio Bank

 Go to Film Bank

 Go to Support section

 Return to home page

Audio Bank

Click on any unit.

A list of all the recordings for that unit will appear on the right side of the screen.

Click on the recording bar  to open the audio player that will play the recording.

You can switch from one section to another using the icons in the bottom navigation bar.

Audio player

Use the slider or the rewind/forward buttons to find a specific part of the audio quickly.
Pressing the Play button while the audio is playing will pause the recording. Pressing the button again will play the recording from the point where it was paused.

Use to control the volume.

Click on 'show' in this panel to view the tapescript of the recording. Hide the tapescript by clicking on the appropriate button. You can print it with or without annotations.

Click here to minimise, maximise or close the audio player window.

Tapescript window

Control the audio using the audio player buttons. Use the small toolbar to control or annotate the tapescript.

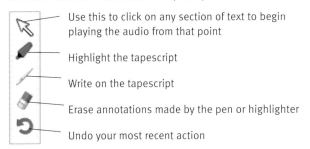

Use this to click on any section of text to begin playing the audio from that point

Highlight the tapescript

Write on the tapescript

Erase annotations made by the pen or highlighter

Undo your most recent action

_|&|×_ Click here to minimise, maximise or close the tapescript window.

Film Bank

In the Film Bank select the unit you are studying.
Click on ![Watch the film] to open the Film Bank player.

You can switch from one section to another using the icons in the bottom navigation bar.

Film Bank player

Use the slider ● ▬▬▬▬▬▬ or the rewind/forward buttons ◄◄ ►► to find a specific part of the video quickly.
Pressing the Play ► button while the video is playing will pause the video. Pressing the button again will play the video from the point where it was paused.
Click subtitles on to turn on the subtitles.
Click subtitles off to turn off the subtitles.

Use ◄·|||||| to control the volume.

Click ![AUDIOSCRIPT SHOW PRINT] to view the video tapescript. Hide or print it by clicking on the appropriate button. You can print the video tapescript with or without annotations. You can also view the English subtitles by clicking on the 'Subtitles on/off' button on this panel.

Film Bank tapescript

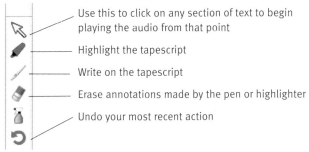

Use this to click on any section of text to begin playing the audio from that point

Highlight the tapescript

Write on the tapescript

Erase annotations made by the pen or highlighter

Undo your most recent action

Click on ![▲ HIDE] to hide the tapescript and return the window to its previous size.

Click here to minimise, maximise or close the Film Bank player
_|&|×_ window.

Students' Book

Click on any unit to open it.

Small pictures of all the double spreads for that unit will appear:

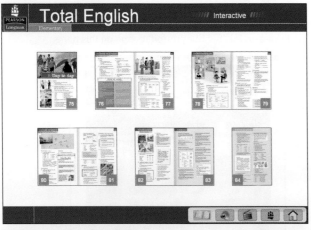

Click on any spread to select it.

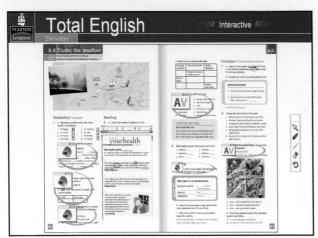

The bottom navigation bar changes to:

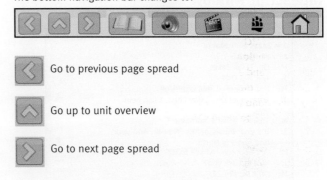

Go to previous page spread

Go up to unit overview

Go to next page spread

Click on any section of the Students' Book page (instructions, pictures, exercises) and it will zoom up to be extra large and easily visible. Click on it again to zoom back out.

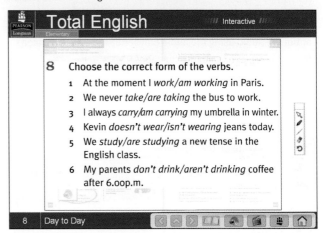

Use the small toolbar to annotate the page spreads or any zoomed-up area

Your annotations will not be saved when you zoom out or change pages.

If a section of the Students' Book is circled, this shows you that there is an either an audio file or an interactive activity for that section. The icon will tell you which one it is: AV, AV for flipcharts and ● for an audio file. Zoom up that section and click on the icon.

The audio recording will behave exactly as it does in the Audio Bank (see page 6).

The flipchart will open in a new window.

What is a flipchart?

Each level of *Total English Digital* includes hundreds of activities specially created to help your students interact directly with the content from the book using interactive whiteboard tools. These interactive activities are called flipcharts. Open a flipchart by clicking on the AV, ◌ ◌ on a zoomed-up part of the page.

AV flipcharts can be used to complete an exercise from the Students' Book using interactive whiteboard tools.

◌ flipcharts contain content *additional* to that in the Students' Book. They encourage further class participation, and have very communicative content.

◌ are Your Ideas flipcharts. These are spaces for brainstorming and class discussion. Notes can easily be made here using ✎ tool.

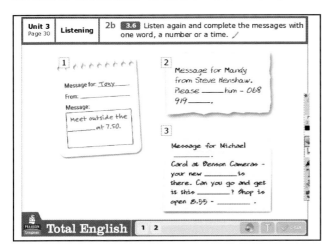

The *Total English Digital* package contains a special type of software called Activstudio (created by one of the leading interactive whiteboard manufacturers, Promethean) that opens a toolbar you can use with the flipcharts no matter what type of interactive whiteboard you have.

The Activstudio toolbar

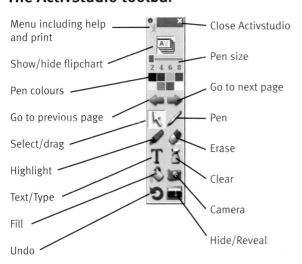

Menu including help and print

Close Activstudio

Show/hide flipchart

Pen size

Pen colours

Go to next page

Go to previous page

Pen

Select/drag

Erase

Highlight

Clear

Text/Type

Camera

Fill

Hide/Reveal

Undo

Other flipchart icons

2.1	Tapescript reference
1 **2**	Go to page 1, 2 etc.
T	Show tapescript/audio player
◉	Play audio
✓ CHECK	Show answers
↻	Reset flipchart
🗑	Rubbish bin (drag any annotations onto this icon to delete them from the flipchart)

The main flipchart activity types

1. ✎ Writing

2. ◔ Erasing

3. ▰ Highlighting

4. ⌖ Drag and drop

The main tools needed for each activity type are shown in the rubric area of the page. Clicking on the icons there or in the toolbar will activate that function, causing the interactive whiteboard pen (or your finger) to act as the selected tool, for example, an eraser or a highlighter.

Within each activity type there are variations on how the tools may be used.

1. ✏ Writing

The flipcharts may require you to use the pen in various ways:
– to write words, phrases or sentences;
– to choose an answer by circling or underlying items;
– to draw lines to match halves of sentences.

2 4 6 8 Use the slider to make the pen width thicker.

■■■■ Use the colour squares to choose a different colour for the 'ink'.

2. ✐ Erasing

Activities that include the eraser will ask you to erase the wrong answer (and leave the correct answer) or to erase a box to reveal the answer.

3. ✐ Highlighting

Highlighting is used in flipchart activities to show stress during pronunciation practice or to emphasize key points.

4. ⬈ Drag and drop

The arrow tool is used in activities to drag words into the correct category to match words or to move the answer into the gap. It is also used to drag a special 'answer box' down the page to reveal the correct answer.

Support section

The support section includes an on-screen user's guide and quick links to further information and support.

Select the unit for the guide you need or one of the general sections on the right. The guide will open in Adobe Acrobat Reader. If you do not have this installed on your computer already, it is free to download from http://www.adobe.com/downloads/.

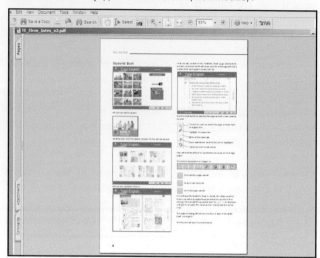

In the support section there is also a link to the *Total English* website where information and material are available.
http:///www.pearsonlongman.com/totalenglish/

FAQ Frequently asked questions

How do I install the software?

When you first insert the CD-ROM into your computer's CD drive, the program will begin to run automatically. It will ask if you want to install or run from CD. Even if you choose to run it directly from the CD-ROM (and are using an interactive whiteboard that is not Promethean brand), you are still required to install Activstudio before *Total English Digital* will work correctly. If you choose to install *Total English Digital*, the program will guide you through the installation.

How do I access Total English Digital?

Go to Start\Programs\Longman and choose your *Total English* level, or click on the desktop icon for the level you want to use.

Is Total English Digital different in any way to the paper edition?

Yes and No. The Students' Book pages contain exactly the same content as the paper edition, so that what your students see on the page is the same as on the screen. In addition, there are direct links to the tapescripts and flipchart activities as well as the Film Bank section. The Film Bank activities, Writing Bank, etc., however, are not included.

How do I access the videos?

You can access the videos directly from the home page when you open the program.

How do I access the Teacher's Book?

A digital copy of the traditional teacher's book is not included; however, unit-by-unit teacher's notes and answer keys for the flipcharts activities are included in this guide.

How do I zoom in/out on a section of the page?

Click on any section of the Students' Book pages, instructions, pictures or exercises, and it will zoom in on the section. Click again to zoom back out.

How do I move forwards and backwards in the Student's Book?

Use ▷ to move to the next page and ◁ to move back a page. If you want to move to another unit, then use ▨ to go back to the overall view of the unit. Click ⌊⏐⌋ to see the list of units.

What do the circles on the page spreads mean?

They show you that there is an interactive activity with this section of the book; either an audio file or a flipchart activity.

How do I write on a Students' Book page?

You can write on a zoomed or unzoomed part of the Students' Book page using the small tools in the toolbar. Alternatively you can use the software that came with your board. For Promethean board users, this would be Activstudio Professional Edition's 'Annotate-over-desktop' functionality. Other board users should consult their hardware manufacturer for advice on how to access similar functionality.

How do my students have access to the Total English Digital from home?

They don't, the digital edition is only licensed to schools and organisations. The software is not designed for students to self-access. A teacher should facilitate the material for them in a classroom environment.

How can I access Total English Digital from home?

Your licence permits you to install *Total English Digital* on teachers' home computers or laptops so they can access the material to prepare their lessons outside the classroom. The software can be controlled from a computer without the interactive whiteboard being plugged in, but some functions, like writing, are considerably more difficult when using a mouse instead of a pen (or finger)!

How do I access the audio file directly without going through the Students' Book pages?

Go to ▨ on the home page and choose the audio file from the unit menu.

Do I still need to use a CD for listening activities?

Most activities include the audio, but, for copyright reasons, you will need to use a CD for any songs in the Students' Book. All listening activities from the Workbook must be played from the CD.

How do I see the tapescript?

Click on ▤ in a flipchart to show the tapescript. If this option does not appear, it is because the tapescript is written out on the page of the flipchart.

In the Audio Bank, click ▤ to make the tapescript and its tools appear. If this option doesn't appear, then there is no tapescript included with this audio file because the tapescript is written out as part of the Students' Book.

How do I cue the audio or video tapescript?

Make sure you have selected ⟡ from the small tapescript toolbar. Then, click on a section of the tapescript (it will change colour) to begin playing from this point. You can use also use the normal pause, fast forward/rewind buttons.

How do I write on a tapescript?

Use the mini toolbar next to the tapescript. Click on ✎ to write, ✐ to highlight, ✦ to erase and ↺ to undo any writing.

How do I make a tapescript bigger?

You can resize the window by dragging a corner or use ▆▆▆ to minimise, maximise or close it.

How do I print a tapescript?

Click the small picture of the printer on the tapescript toolbar.

Where are the flipcharts?

You can see the ▆ icon on the double spread or enlarged section of your Students' Book. Click on it to launch the flipchart activity.

How do I check the answers to activities?

Select ▆▆▆ . Sometimes you can check one by one, or sometimes the whole page at once.

How do I get rid of the flipchart answers?

If showing answers is the last thing you have done, click on ↺ to undo your last step. Otherwise close the flipchart and reopen it to reset the page.

How do I know where the answers are going to appear on the page?

Before you use the page with your students, click on ▆▆▆ to see where the answer boxes appear or consult the unit-by-unit notes in this guide. Then make sure you or your students don't write in that area.

How do I write on a flipchart?

Use ✎ from the Activstudio tool bar or click on the ✎ next to the activity instructions.

How do I erase what I've written?

For individual words or small sections, use the ✦ from the Activstudio tool bar.

How do I reset the page to its original state?

Close the flipchart and reopen it to reset the page.

How do I switch between the flipchart and the Students' Book?

Click on ▆ at the top of your Activstudio toolbar to temporarily hide the flipchart and take you back to the Student's Book. Click on ▆ again to bring back your flipchart.

How do I edit or save changes to flipcharts? Can I add my own pictures or text?

You can save any changes you make in a flipchart. Click on the orange figure on the Activstudio toolbar and select 'Flipchart' then 'Save As'. You will need to select a place on your computer to save it. Your saved version will not be opened through the page spreads. You will need to open it from where you saved it.

If you want to create your own flipchart to add pictures or text, you can use your board's own software or choose Flipchart/New from the menu under the orange figure on the Activstudio toolbar.

How do I keep a blank flipchart page open for my own notes?

If you are using the edition of Activstudio that came with *Total English Digital*, you can only have one flipchart open at a time, but you could always switch between a blank page of a Word document or a flipchart in your interactive whiteboard's native software.

If you are using Activstudio Professional Edition then you can have your own flipcharts open at the same time as a *Total English Digital* flipchart. Click on ▆ 'Arrange windows' icon in the top right of your screen to switch between the two flipcharts.

How do I close a flipchart?

Close the Activstudio software by clicking on the cross ▆▆▆ on the toolbar.

The program will ask you if you want to save your changes. You may save over the original version of the flipchart or save a changed version elsewhere on your computer.

Click on **page 5**. It will expand to fill the screen. Remember, you can zoom in to any part of the page by clicking on it, and return by clicking on it again.

Try this with the pictures on p5.

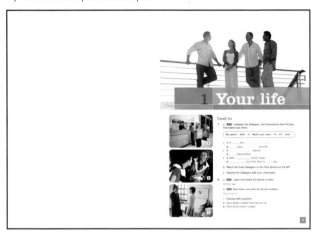

Flipchart: *Lead-In* **p5**

Open the flipchart by clicking on the circled area and then on the flipchart button Ⓐⱽ.

1a Students look at the dialogues in their books and use the expressions from the box to try to complete the sentences. Students check answers in pairs.

Click on the arrow button ⸙ and ask students to tell you their answers. Click on the words in the box above and drag them to the appropriate place in the dialogues. There are several copies of the words.

Click on the audio button 🔊 at the bottom of the screen to play recording 1.1 so that students can see if they were correct. A small window will open and the audio will start playing immediately. You can adjust the volume using the slider in the bottom right of the audio window.

Pause if necessary, by clicking on the slider and repeat if necessary by dragging the slider back (or you can click on the pause button and then on play to resume).

> **TIP:** *You can move the audio window to a different place on the screen by clicking on the title bar and dragging the window to the desired location.*

b Students match the three dialogues to the photos in their book with a partner.

Click on the pen button ✎ and ask students to tell you which numbers to write in the boxes next to the pictures.

> **TIP:** *Click on the slider below* Ⓐⱽ *in the toolbar to change the width of the pen.*

To reveal all the answers, click on the green tick check button ✓ at the bottom. The answers will be displayed in green boxes following the dialogues. The picture numbers will be displayed to the left of the white boxes.

c Students practise saying the dialogues to each other.

Close the flipchart by clicking X in the toolbar.
Return to the double spread by clicking on the zoomed-up area to make it smaller.
Click on ⏵ to go to the next double spread.

Double Spread p6/7

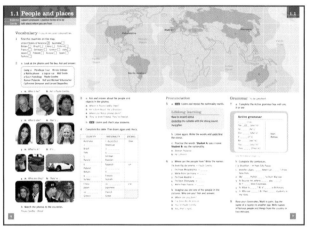

Flipchart: *Your ideas* **p6**

Open the flipchart by clicking on the circled area and then on the Your Ideas button Ⓐⱽ.

Use this area to collate ideas from your students.

Ask students to look at the map on pages 6–7 in their books or the smaller version on the flipchart. Ask them to brainstorm all the countries and cities they can think of. Use the pen tool ✎ to write their ideas into the correct columns.

Close the flipchart by clicking X in the toolbar.
Return to the double spread by clicking on the zoomed-up area to make it smaller.

Flipchart: *Vocabulary* **p6**

Open the flipchart by clicking on the circled area and then on Ⓐⱽ.

2a Because of the length, this exercise is on two pages ①
and ②.

Ask students to look at the four questions in their books. With a partner, students then identify the people from the names in the box by asking and answering the questions.

Click on ⸙ and ask a student to come to the interactive whiteboard. Get them to point at a picture, ask the appropriate question to the group and drag the answer from the box at the top. Ask the student to place the names *below* the pictures (as the answers will be displayed in boxes next to the pictures). Either continue or ask the student to choose another classmate to come up to the board.

Click on ② to move to the next questions 3 and 4, and continue. Click on the left pointing arrow ◀ in the toolbar to return to the previous page ①. Alternatively, you can click ① at the bottom. To check your answers, click on ▭ at the bottom of each page.

ANSWERS
1 Paulo Coelho; Will Smith; Roman Polanski 2 Penelope Cruz; Gong Li; Nicole Kidman 3 a Nokia phone; a Gucci handbag; a Jaguar car 4 Catherine Deneuve and Gerard Depardieu 5 Ralf and Michael Schumacher

Close the flipchart by clicking X in the toolbar.
Return to the double spread by clicking on the zoomed-up area to make it smaller.

Flipchart: *Pronunciation* **p7**
Open the flipchart by clicking on the circled area and then on ▭.
3a Click on ▭ in the top left corner to play recording 1.5. Students listen and repeat the nationality words. Pay particular attention to Italian and Chinese as the word stress changes in the adjective form for these.
b Click on ✎ and write Australian on the interactive whiteboard. Say: *Australian*, enunciating each syllable clearly (Aus-tral-ian). Ask: *How many syllables are there?* (three) *Where is the stress?* (tral, syllable two). Underline the stressed syllable on the interactive whiteboard. Click on ▭ to play the recording again. Students listen and write the words in their books, underlining the stressed syllable as they do so. Students check in pairs.
Ask a student to come to the interactive whiteboard and write the nationality words and underline the stress. Encourage the student to ask the group if they agree with the spelling and to ask for the number of syllables and the stress.

> **TIP:** *If students make a mistake, click on the Undo button ↺ in the toolbar to delete the last pen stroke. Alternatively, click on the eraser button ✐ and you can rub out part of the last stroke.*

To check your answers, click on ▭ at the bottom. The answers will be displayed in a box in the bottom right corner.

ANSWERS
A̲u̲s̲tralian A̲me̲rican Bra̲zi̲lian I̲talian Ge̲rman R̲ussian S̲panish P̲olish B̲ritish T̲urkish F̲innish Chine̲se Japane̲se French Greek

Close the flipchart by clicking X in the toolbar.
Return to the double spread by clicking on the zoomed-up area to make it smaller.
Click on ▷ to go to the next double spread.

Double Spread p8/9

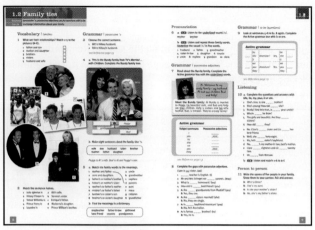

Flipchart: *Grammar* **p8**
Open the flipchart by clicking on the circled area and then on ▭.
4a Students complete the family tree in their books in pairs. Ask a student to come to the interactive whiteboard, click on ✎ and write in the names.
To check your answers, click on ▭ at the bottom.

ANSWERS
Al = Peggy; Kelly – Bud

Click on ② to move to exercise 4b.
b Students use the 's to make sentences about the family and check in pairs.
Click on ✎, elicit the first sentence as an example and write it up on the interactive whiteboard.
Ask a student to come to the interactive whiteboard and write a sentence for each word. Ask that student to choose another student to write.
To check your answers, click on ▭ to display them all on a new page.

ANSWERS
Al is Peggy's husband. Peggy is Al's wife. Kelly is Bud's sister. Bud is Kelly's brother. Peggy is Kelly and Bud's mother. Al is Kelly and Bud's father. Kelly is Al and Peggy's daughter. Bud is Al and Peggy's son.

Click on ▨ at the bottom to return to ② to compare your answers.

> **TIP:** *Use a different colour pen for correction by clicking on one of the coloured squares in the toolbar*

> **TIP:** *Click on ✐ in the toolbar and highlight the words for males. Change the colour by clicking on a different coloured square in the toolbar and highlight the words for females. Ask the students which colours to choose.*

Click on ③ to move to exercise 5a.
5a In their books, students match the family words to the meanings and check in pairs. Click on ▹ and ask a student to come to the interactive whiteboard and drag the family words up or down in the column on the right to match the meanings.

TIP: *Drag and 'park' temporarily unwanted words on top of the lines to avoid overwriting.*

To check your answers, click on [IMG] at the bottom to display them on a new page.

ANSWERS
1 d 2 g 3 a 4 e 5 b 6 h 7 c 8 f

TIP: *For further practice at this point (or later, as revision), on the answers page click on ✎ , choose a thick pen width and blank out all the family words. Now, click on 🖐 and ask a student to come up to the interactive whiteboard, say what the words are and use the eraser to reveal the words. If students cannot remember, erase only part of the word to help them. Use the opportunity to check spelling, too.*

Close the flipchart by clicking X in the toolbar.
Return to the double spread by clicking on the zoomed-up area to make it smaller.

Flipchart: *Grammar* p9

Open the flipchart by clicking on the circled area and then on [AV].
9 Students focus on their completed questions from Ex. 8 and use them to complete the Active grammar box in their books using either *is* or *are* in the spaces provided. Students check in pairs. Click on ✎ and ask students to come to the interactive whiteboard and write the verbs to complete the box.
To check your answers, click on [IMG] at the bottom to display the answers in boxes at the sides.

ANSWERS
Is is Are are

TIP: *Use different colours for is and are.*

Click on [2].
10a Students focus on the dialogue between two people, one asking questions about a photograph and the other answering. Students complete the dialogue in their books with *she, he, my, your, is, 's or are*. Click on ✎ and ask a student to come to the interactive whiteboard and write the missing words along the lines.
b Click on [IMG] to play recording 1.8. Students check and match the questions 1–6 to the answers a–f.
To check your answers, click on [IMG] at the bottom.

ANSWERS
1 your 2 is 3 he 4 is 5 your 6 are a my, is b 's c my d she e 's, 's f 's

ANSWERS
1 d 2 b 3 c 4 f 5 a 6 e

Close the flipchart by clicking X in the toolbar.
Return to the double spread by clicking on the zoomed-up area to make it smaller.
Click on [IMG] to go to the next double spread.

Double Spread p10/11

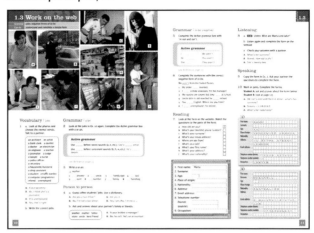

Flipchart: *Vocabulary* p10

Open the flipchart by clicking on the circled area and then on [AV].
1b Because of the length, this exercise is on two pages [1] and [2] .
Students look at the photos in their books with a partner and match the job to the correct photo. Click on [↖] and ask a student to come to the interactive whiteboard and drag an appropriate job onto the photo. Click on [2] to move to the rest of the photos. Click on [1] to return.
To check your answers, click on [IMG] to display them in boxes below or next to the photos. Click on [2] and repeat. Alternatively, you can check your answers as soon as you have finished the first page, before doing the second.

ANSWERS
A a journalist B a police officer C a doctor D a lawyer E a computer programmer F an architect G a shop assistant H unemployed I an electrician

Close the flipchart by clicking X in the toolbar.
Return to the double spread by clicking on the zoomed-up area to make it smaller.

Flipchart: *Reading* p11

Open the flipchart by clicking on the circled area and then on [AV].
7 Point to the form on the interactive whiteboard and establish that it is *an application form*. Ask: Where is this form? (on a website on the Internet). Elicit the types of questions found on forms (name, address, etc.).
Students look at the questions in their books. In pairs, they match them to the parts of the form.
Click on ✎ and ask a student to come to the interactive whiteboard and write the numbers in the boxes to match the questions and information.
To check your answers, click on [IMG] to display them at the side of the boxes.

ANSWERS
a 3 b 8 c 2 d 7 e 4 f 9 g 1 h 6 i 5

TIP: *Click on ✎ and use different colours to highlight some of the more difficult vocabulary (a, e, f, c)*

TIP: *Use the reveal tool to hide the questions. Click on* 🔲 *and the screen will be covered with a black blind. Drag the pointer from the bottom right quarter to the left and reveal the form. See if students can remember the questions and then drag the blind to the left to reveal them. Click on* 🔲 *again to remove the reveal tool.*

Click on 2 to move to the listening exercise 8.

8a Click on 🔊 in the top left corner to play recording 1.9 once. Students listen to find out who the two people are. Tell them you will play the recording a second time in a minute. Click on 🖊 and ask students to tell you what to write on the line. Click on ▭▭ at the end of the first line to display the answer below the line.

ANSWER
Marta and Jake attend the same English class in London.

b Play the recording again. This time students listen for the details and fill in the form in Ex. 7 in their books. Repeat any parts of the listening as required.

Students check in pairs.

Click on 🖊 and ask a student to come to the interactive whiteboard to complete the form.

To check your answers, click on ▭▭ next to the form to display them at the side of the form.

ANSWERS
2 Nowak 3 22 4 Lublin, Poland 5 Polish 6 36,
Mill Lane, London 7 marta.nowak@hotserve.com
8 020 87306589 (home) 03743 5485 132 (mobile)
9 student

Close the flipchart by clicking X in the toolbar.

Return to the double spread by clicking on the zoomed-up area to make it smaller.

Click on ≫ to go to the next double spread.

Flipchart: *Special flipchart* p10
Open the flipchart by clicking on the circled area and then on the Special Flipchart button 🔲.

Because of length the exercise is on three pages 1 2 and 3

To prompt student discussion, use the eraser tool to show small sections of the two boxes. Click on the eraser tool and drag it over the box.

Ask students to suggest jobs based on what they see. You can use the pen tool 🖊 to write down any ideas the students can come up with.

To reveal the answers click on the check button ▭▭ at the bottom.

Click on 2 and 3 to finish the exercise.

ANSWERS:
taxi driver, porter, plumber, journalist, hairdresser, secretary

Close the flipchart by clicking X in the toolbar.

Return to the double spread by clicking on the zoomed-up area to make it smaller.

Flipchart: *Your ideas* p11
Open the flipchart by clicking on the circled area and then on the Your Ideas button 🔲.

Use this area to collate ideas from your students.

Using the pen tool 🖊 write down as many interview questions as your class can think of. See if the students can answer any of the questions.

Close the flipchart by clicking X in the toolbar.

Return to the double spread by clicking on the zoomed-up area to make it smaller.

Double Spread p12/13

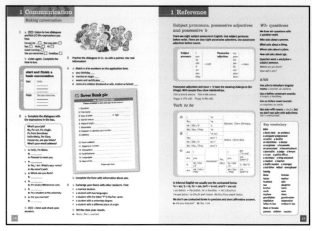

Flipchart: *Making conversation* p12
Open the flipchart by clicking on the circled area and then on 🔲.

Click on 🔲 to hide the flipchart.

1a Elicit from students all the ways they know of saying *hello* and *goodbye* in English.

Click on 🔲 again to reveal the flipchart and ask students to check if they mentioned all the ones there. Click on 🔊 and play recording 1.10. Students tick the expressions they hear in their books and check answers in pairs. Click on 🖊 and ask a student to come to the interactive whiteboard to tick the expressions they heard.

To check your answers, click on ▭▭ at the bottom.

ANSWERS
Excuse me; See you later; Bye; Hi; Good morning; Goodbye.

Click on 2 .

b Students listen again and complete the *How To...* box in their books and check in pairs. Click on 🖊 and ask a student to come to the interactive whiteboard to complete the *How To...* box.

To check your answers, click on ▭▭ to display them at the side of the box.

ANSWERS
Start: Hello Excuse me Hi Good morning. Finish: See you tomorrow See you later Bye Goodbye

Click on 🖊 and ask students to use different colours to categorise the words into three groups: *informal*, *formal* and *both*. Discuss the different categories with the students.

Close the flipchart by clicking X in the toolbar.

Return to the double spread by clicking on the zoomed-up area to make it smaller.

Click on the upwards pointing arrow 🔲 to return to the contents page in order to go to the next module.

Click on **page 15**.

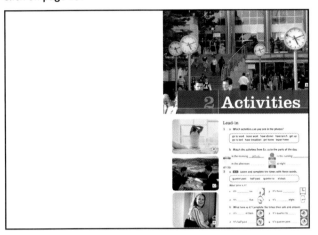

Flipchart: *Lead-in* **p15**

Open the flipchart by clicking on the circled area and then on AV .

2a Click on [icon] at the bottom of the page so that students can listen to recording 2.1 and write the correct times in their books. Students check answers with a partner. Click on [icon] in the toolbar or in the rubric and ask a student to come to the interactive whiteboard and drag the words from the top onto the lines to complete the times next to the correct clock.

Click on [icon] and ask a student to erase the purple boxes to reveal the correct times beneath.

Alternatively, you can click on [icon] to reveal the answers in the boxes below the times.

> **ANSWERS**
> 1 half past 2 quarter to 3 o'clock 4 quarter past

Click on [2] .

b Students look at the clock faces, write the times in their books and work with a partner (ask and answer) to find out what times each has written down. Click on [icon], either in the toolbar or in the rubric, and ask a student to come to the interactive whiteboard to write on the lines to complete the times.

You can either check each time as you work through by clicking on the small individual [icon] s after the clocks, or check them all together at the end by clicking on the larger [icon] at the bottom.

> **ANSWERS**
> 1 two 2 ten 3 twelve 4 one

Click on [3] to show the interactive clock.

Click on the clock to open it in a new window.

Possible activities:

Ask two students to come to the interactive whiteboard. Click on [icon] and one student drags the hands of the clock. Click on [icon], and the other student has to write the time. If more space is needed, click on [icon] to move to a new page. The clock window will remain open. This could work as a team game.

The digital time can be hidden if not required.

For speaking practice, you can maximise the clock window to fill the screen by clicking next to the X in the blue menu bar of its window. Click on restore to return to the original size.

One student comes to the interactive whiteboard, students shout out a time and he/she has to drag the clock hands to show the correct time.

Alternatively, the student at the board can select the time and ask one of the class what time it is.

> **TIP:** *Remember to return to this page in the future for revision of telling the time.*

Close the flipchart by clicking X in the toolbar.

Return to the double spread by clicking on the zoomed-up area to make it smaller.

Flipchart: *Special flipchart* **p15**

Open the flipchart by clicking on the circled area and then on the Special Flipchart button [icon].

This flipchart contains a link to an interactive extra. The resource is a clock with moveable hands that you can use to consolidate what has been taught in the lesson (or, alternatively, you can use it at the beginning or throughout the lesson to establish how much/how little your students already know about telling the time).

You can use the clock in two ways. One is to move the hands around, using the Select Tool, and the correct time will show up on the digital clock. The digital display can be hidden or shown, depending on the task. You can also type the time into the digital display and the large clock will show the time you ask for.

Close the flipchart by clicking X in the toolbar.

Return to the double spread by clicking on the zoomed-up area to make it smaller.

Click on [icon] to go to the next double spread.

Double Spread p16/17

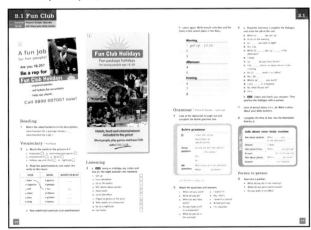

Flipchart: *Listening* **p16**

Open the flipchart by clicking on the circled area and then on AV

3a Explain to students that only eight activities are mentioned, two are not. (They are in the correct order). Click on [icon] to play recording 2.2. In their books, students tick the activities mentioned as they listen. Students check answers in pairs.

TIP: *Drag the audio window to the side, so that it is not covering the boxes. You can also drag the* AV *toolbar to move it to a more convenient location if you want to.*

Click on ✏ and ask a student to come to the interactive whiteboard and draw two crosses in the boxes next to the two activities not mentioned.
Click on ✔ to check the answers. The ticks will be displayed next to the boxes.

ANSWERS
2 Have breakfast and 6 Go to the office are not mentioned.

Click on 2 .
b Students look at Jenny's diary. Click on 🔊 to play the recording again. Students listen and complete the diaries in their books by filling in the times and activities mentioned.
Click on ⤺ and ask a student to come to the interactive whiteboard and drag the first activity into the space in the diary. Ask them to click on ✏ and write the time next to it. Ask for help from the class if necessary. Click on ⤺ again and continue, with different students if appropriate.
Click on ✔ to display the answers on a new page. Click on ⌃ to return to 2 to compare answers.

ANSWERS
2 about eleven 3 quarter past eleven 4 2 o'clock
5 half past three 6 quarter to eight 7 half past ten
8 half past one

Close the flipchart by clicking X in the toolbar.
Return to the double spread by clicking on the zoomed-up area to make it smaller.

Flipchart: *Grammar* **p17**
Open the flipchart by clicking on the circled area and then on AV
5 Students match the questions to the answers in their books. Do the first one as a whole class. Click on ⤺ and ask students to tell you which answer to move. Drag the answers up and down in their column. Remember, you can ask a student to come to the interactive whiteboard and drag the answers to their correct position.
Click on ✔ to display the answers on a new page.
Click on ⌃ to return to 1 to compare answers.

ANSWERS
1 c 2 e 3 d 4 b 5 a

TIP: *For further practice, on the answer page, click on* ✏ *, drag the slider to increase the width and using red (for example) ask a student to come to the interactive whiteboard and blank out all the questions. Then students can see if they can remember them. Click on* 🧽 *and erase the red to reveal the questions again. This can be done slowly to give students clues if they are having difficulty remembering.*

Help students with the pronunciation of the questions, especially the weak /ə/ sound of the auxiliary verb *do*. Students practise asking and answering these questions in pairs. Monitor closely and correct mistakes.

Close the flipchart by clicking X in the toolbar.
Return to the double spread by clicking on the zoomed-up area to make it smaller.

Flipchart: *Grammar* **p17**
Open the flipchart by clicking on the circled area and then on AV
8 Students complete the *How to...* box in their books, using the language and information from their completed Ex. 6. Students check in pairs. Click on ✏ and ask a student to come to the interactive whiteboard to write in the missing words.
Click on ✔ to display the answers in boxes at the side.

ANSWERS
do/do do At do work

Close the flipchart by clicking X in the toolbar.
Return to the double spread by clicking on the zoomed-up area to make it smaller.

Flipchart: *Your ideas* **p17**
Open the flipchart by clicking on the circled area and then on the Your Ideas button 💭 .
Use this area to collate ideas from your students.
Ask students to think of what they do in an average day. Using the pen tool ✏ write down their suggestions.
Close the flipchart by clicking X in the toolbar.
Return to the double spread by clicking on the zoomed-up area to make it smaller.

Click on ⧸⧸ to go to the next double spread.

Double Spread p18/19

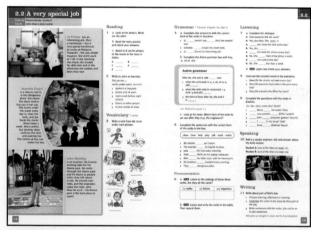

Flipchart: *Vocabulary* **p18**
Open the flipchart by clicking on the circled area and then on AV
3 Students work in pairs. They match verbs from the reading texts to the pictures in their books. Click on ✏ and ask a student to come to the interactive whiteboard to write the verbs under each picture.
Click on ✔ to display the answers in boxes at the side of the page.

ANSWERS
a walk b swim c watch d wash e listen f feed g invent.

TIP: *If necessary, use a different colour pen for correction by clicking on one of the coloured squares in the toolbar.*

Close the flipchart by clicking X in the toolbar.
Return to the double spread by clicking on the zoomed-up area to make it smaller.

Flipchart: *Listening* **p19**
Open the flipchart by clicking on the circled area and then on A∨
8 Tell students to use their completed dialogue from exercise 7 to help them choose the correct form in their books. They cross out the incorrect words in the questions.
The first one is done for them as an example. Click on 🧽 and ask students to tell you what to erase in 1.
Students check in pairs. Ask a student to come to the interactive whiteboard and erase the incorrect choices.
Click on ▭ to highlight the answers.
You can either check each question as you work through by clicking on the individual ▭s at the end of the line or check all the questions together at the end by clicking on ▭ at the bottom.

ANSWERS
2 Do/cleans 3 Do/likes

Click on 2 .
9 Students complete the questions in their books using the correct form of the verbs. The first one is done for them.
Click on ✎ and ask a student to come to the interactive whiteboard to write the words in the gaps to complete the questions.
Click on ▭ to display the answers in boxes below the lines.
Again, depending on your class, you can either check each question as you work through by clicking on the individual ▭ s at the end of the line or check all the questions together at the end by clicking on ▭ at the bottom.

ANSWERS
1 Does/like 2 Do/watch 3 Does/invent 4 Do/talk
5 Does/have

Close the flipchart by clicking X in the toolbar.
Return to the double spread by clicking on the zoomed-up area to make it smaller.

Flipchart: *Your ideas* **p18**
Open the flipchart by clicking on the circled area and then on the *Your Ideas* button ⸫ .
This page is to be used to record suggestions from your students.
Ask students what they do at work (or at college/school) and use the pen tool ✎ to write down any ideas.
Close the flipchart by clicking X in the toolbar.
Return to the double spread by clicking on the zoomed-up area to make it smaller.

Click on ▦ to go to the next double spread.

Double Spread p20/21

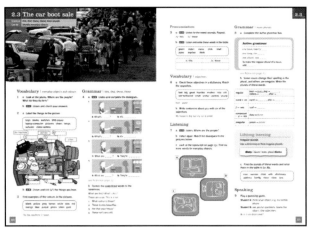

Flipchart: *Vocabulary* **p20**
Open the flipchart by clicking on the circled area and then on A∨
2a Students look at the picture and see if they know the names for any of the items. They then label the objects in their books in pairs.
Click on ⌐ and ask a student to come to the interactive whiteboard and drag the words from the top into the boxes to label the picture correctly.
Click on ▭ to display the answers on a new page.
Click on ◀ to return to 1 to compare labels.

TIP: *Nominate students to be responsible for checking individual numbers. Alternatively, click on ✎ and highlight the doubtful numbers that need to be checked.*

ANSWERS
1 books 2 watches 3 lamps 4 suitcase 5 DVD player
6 video camera 7 laptop computer 8 bags
9 pictures 10 shoes

TIP: *If students need additional practice of this vocabulary, click on ▬ and drag the sheet up so that it is covering the vocabulary in the box at the top. Click on ✎ and ask students to come up to the interactive whiteboard and write in the labels. Click on ▬ to remove the sheet and check as before.*

Click on 2 .
b Click on 🔘 so that students can listen to recording 2.8 and tick the items they hear in their books. Check answers in pairs. Click on ✎ and ask a student to come to the interactive whiteboard and tick the items heard. Ask the group for help if necessary.
Click on ▭ to display the ticks next to the boxes.

ANSWERS
laptop, watches, shoes, lamps, suitcase

Close the flipchart by clicking X in the toolbar.
Return to the double spread by clicking on the zoomed-up area to make it smaller.

Flipchart: *Listening* **p21**

Open the flipchart by clicking on the circled area and then on AV

7a Students close their books. Teach *Madam* and *Sir* as a way of addressing people in a formal or official situation. Ask them to listen to the three dialogues and find out where the people are.

Click on ▣ in the top left corner and play recording 2.12. Students check answers in pairs. Click on ⟋ and ask a student to come to the interactive whiteboard and write along the line where the people are.

Click on ▣ at the end of the question to display the answer.

> **ANSWER**
> At the security bag check at an airport.

b Students look at the pictures in their books. They identify the objects in the bags with a partner. Click on ▣ to play the recording again. Alternatively, you can play each dialogue separately by clicking on the ▣ next to each picture. Students listen and match each dialogue to the correct picture in their books. Check answers in pairs. Click on ⟨ and ask a student to come to the interactive whiteboard and drag the dialogue box below the correct picture of the suitcase.

Click on ▣ to display the answers below the lines.

> **ANSWERS**
> A DIALOGUE 2; B DIALOGUE 1; C DIALOGUE 3

Click on 2 .

In pairs, students check the tapescript to find six more words for everyday objects. Click on ⟋ and ask a student to come to the interactive whiteboard and write the words along the lines provided.

Click on ▣ to display the answers in a box on the right.

> **ANSWERS**
> Digital camera, discs, laptop, magazines, wallet, scissors.

Close the flipchart by clicking X in the toolbar.

Return to the double spread by clicking on the zoomed-up area to make it smaller.

Click on the upwards pointing arrow ▣ to return to Unit 2, and then on ▣ to return to the contents page to go to the next module.

Click on **page 25.**

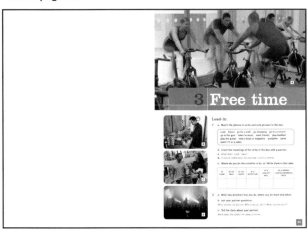

Flipchart: *Your ideas* **p25**

Open the flipchart by clicking on the circled area and then on the Your Ideas button .

Use this area to collate ideas from your students.

Ask the students to go in to more detail about what they like to do in their spare time. Use the pen tool ✏ to make notes. Remember that you can print the class notes direct from the flipchart.

Close the flipchart by clicking X in the toolbar.

Return to the double spread by clicking on the zoomed-up area to make it smaller.

Flipchart: *Lead-in* **p25**

Open the flipchart by clicking on the circled area and then on A✓.

1a In pairs, students look at the photos in their books and choose verbs and verb phrases in the box that describe them. Click on ⌕ and ask a student to come to the interactive whiteboard and drag the verbs from the box in the middle to an area above the photos.

To check the answers, click on ✓CHECK to display the answers on a new page.

Click on ⌂ to return to 1 to compare your answers.

> **ANSWERS**
> A go to the gym B cook C go shopping D go to a concert

Click on 2 .

b Direct students to the verbs in the box and ask them to check the words they don't know with a partner.

> **TIP:** *Click on ✏ and highlight the following combinations to focus students' attention on the use of the definite and indefinite article: go to a concert/ go to the gym; play football/play the guitar; watch TV/ watch a video; listen to music/listen to the radio.*

Click on ✏ and ask a student to come to the interactive whiteboard and write some example exchanges like the one in the book.

Click on 3 .

c In pairs, students organise the words according to the table. There will be some overlap between the categories. Encourage students to discuss these. Click on ⌕ and ask a student to come

to the interactive whiteboard to drag the verbs from the top into appropriate columns.

Encourage students to add as many activities as they can to the list.

To check the answers, click on ✓CHECK to display the answers on a new page.

Click on ⌂ to return to 3 to compare.

> **POSSIBLE ANSWERS**
> At home: cook, listen to music, play the guitar, read a book or magazine, sunbathe, watch TV or a video; In the park: listen to music, go for a walk, meet friends, go to a concert, play the guitar, read a book or magazine, sunbathe, play football; At the shops: go shopping, meet friends; At a nightclub: dance, meet friends, listen to music; At a concert hall: dance, go to a concert, listen to music, meet friends; At a sports centre/swimming pool: go to the gym, listen to music, meet friends, play football, sunbathe, read a book or magazine, swim

Close the flipchart by clicking X in the toolbar.

Return to the double spread by clicking on the zoomed-up area to make it smaller.

Click on ▷ to go to the next double spread.

Double Spread p26/27

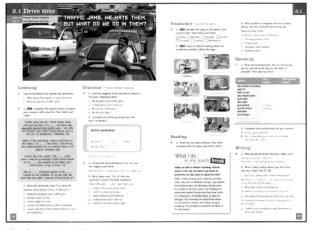

Flipchart: *Listening* **p26**

Open the flipchart by clicking on the circled area and then on A✓.

2a This exercise is on pages 1 and 2 .

Tell students they are going to listen to five people talking about what they do in traffic jams. Students read through the texts in their books first and try to guess what the missing words/phrases might be. They check ideas with a partner. Click on 🔊 to play recording 3.1 once and students listen to see if they were right.

Click on ✏ and ask a student to come to the interactive whiteboard and write the words along the lines to complete the quotes.

TIP: *If necessary, play the audio again and repeat the missing parts by dragging the slider back a little way and then releasing.*

You can either check each page as you finish or click on **2**, finish the exercise and then click on **1** to return and check all the answers together at the end.

To check the answers, click on ▭ to display the answers in boxes below the lines.

ANSWERS
1 write 2 listen to 3 hate 4 watch 5 play 6 call

Click on **3**.

b Students cover the reading text and then read the five sentences. Click on ▭ to play the recording again.

Students listen to see if the statements are true or false and mark in their books. After listening, students check answers with a partner.

Click on / and ask a student to come to the interactive whiteboard and write T or F in the boxes.

To check the answers, click on ▭ to display the answers next to the boxes.

ANSWERS
1 F 2 F 3 T 4 F 5 F

Close the flipchart by clicking X in the toolbar.

Return to the double spread by clicking on the zoomed-up area to make it smaller.

Flipchart: *Your ideas* p27

Open the flipchart by clicking on the circled area and then on the Your Ideas button ▭.

Use this area to collate ideas from your students.

Ask the students to talk about what they do during their lunch breaks. Use the pen tool / to make notes. Remember that you can print the class notes directly from the flipchart.

Close the flipchart by clicking X in the toolbar.

Return to the double spread by clicking on the zoomed-up area to make it smaller.

Click on ▭ to go to the next double spread.

Double Spread p28/29

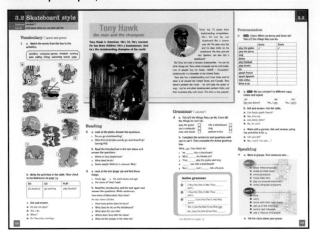

Flipchart: *Vocabulary* p28

Open the flipchart by clicking on the circled area and then on ▭.

1a This exercise is on **1** and **2**.

In their books, students focus on the pictures and match them to an activity in the box. Students check in pairs.

Click on ▭ and ask a student to come to the interactive whiteboard to drag the words from the middle onto the lines below the pictures.

You can either check the answers for each page as you finish or click on **2**, finish the exercise and then click on **1** to return and check all the answers together at the end.

To check the answers, click on ▭ to display the answers below the lines.

ANSWERS
A football B yoga C sailing D aerobics E running F computer games G judo H skiing I swimming J tennis

TIP: *Click on / and ask students to use different colours to categorise the words into (1) indoor/outdoor activities and (2) activities which we do alone/in teams.*

TIP: *For revision, now or later, click on /, select a thick width, and blank out the words in the box in the middle. Select a thinner width and ask students to come to the interactive whiteboard and label the activities. Check as before.*

Click on **3**.

b Students complete the table in their books and check answers with a partner. Click on ▭ and ask a student to come to the interactive whiteboard and drag the words into the correct columns.

TIP: *Click on / and highlight the three columns in different colours to help students visualise and remember the combinations. Draw students' attention to the fact that play is usually used with activities done in teams or games. Do is usually used with non-game activities which we do alone. Ask students what they notice about what is usually used with go (the -ing form of the verb).*

To check the answers, click on ▭ to display the answers in boxes below the columns.

ANSWERS
DO: yoga, judo, aerobics, GO: sailing, swimming, skiing, running PLAY: computer games, tennis, football

Close the flipchart by clicking X in the toolbar.

Return to the double spread by clicking on the zoomed-up area to make it smaller.

Flipchart: *Grammar* p29

Open the flipchart by clicking on the circled area and then on ▭.

4a Say: *Tony can ride a skateboard* and then click on ▭ and highlight it in the list on the interactive whiteboard. Ask: *Is he good at skateboarding?* Elicit if anyone else likes skateboarding. Find a student (or yourself) who doesn't skateboard. Click on /

and write: *X (name of person) can't skateboard* on the interactive whiteboard. Establish that X is not good at it.

Students cover the text in their books and, with a partner, try to remember what Tony can and can't do. They look at the list of activities in Ex. 4a and in pairs mark a ✓ next to what he can do and an × next to what he can't do. Students check their answers in the text. Click on ✎ and ask a student to come to the interactive whiteboard to write a tick or cross in the boxes.

To check the answers, click on ▨ to display the answers after the boxes.

> **ANSWERS**
> play the guitar ✗ use a computer ✓ play rock music ✗
> ride a skateboard ✓ sing ✗ perform tricks ✓

Click on ②.

b Students complete the sentences/questions in their books using *can* and *can't*. Students check in pairs.

Click on ✎ and ask a student to come to the interactive whiteboard to write *can* or *can't* on the lines to complete the questions/sentences.

To check the answers, click on ▨ to display the answers at the end of the sentences/questions.

> **ANSWERS**
> 1 can 2 can 3 can 4 can't 5 Can 6 can't, can

Click on ③.

Students complete the Active grammar box in their books.

Click on ✎ and ask a student to come to the interactive whiteboard to write on the lines to complete the Active Grammar box.

Ask students if they notice anything different about the verb can: It never changes, (no s after He/She can); It doesn't need another verb to make it negative or to ask a question (I don't can swim. Do you can swim?); It almost always has another verb with it (I can swim). Click on ✐ to highlight these points for the students. Direct students to the reference section on page 33 of their books.

To check the answers, click on ▨ to display the answers at the end of the rows.

> **ANSWERS**
> can can't can can't

Close the flipchart by clicking X in the toolbar.

Return to the double spread by clicking on the zoomed-up area to make it smaller.

Click on ▷ to go to the next double spread.

Double Spread p30/31

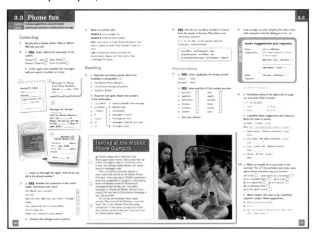

Flipchart: *Listening p30*

Open the flipchart by clicking on the circled area and then on Ａ⍟.

b This exercise is on ① and ②.

Students read through the written messages in their books. Click on 🔊 to play the first part of recording 3.6 again. Students complete the texts for the first three messages in their books with the missing words and check answers in pairs. Click on ✎ and ask a student to come to the interactive whiteboard and write on the lines to complete the messages. Check the answers for ① by clicking on ▨ before clicking on ② to continue.

Click on 🔊 and play the second part of the audio for messages 4 and 5. Students complete in their books and check with a partner. Click on ✎ Ask a student to come to the interactive whiteboard and write on the lines to complete the messages.

c Drag the slider in the audio window to play message 5 again to check the number. Ask students to check with a partner and then ask students to tell you what to write for 88.

To check the answers, click on ▨ to display the answers in boxes next to the lines.

> **ANSWERS**
> 1 Jane, cinema 2 call, -0752 3 Brown, camera, week,
> 6.30 4 dinner, Italian, office 5 David, 391, call
> 2c double eight

Close the flipchart by clicking X in the toolbar.

Return to the double spread by clicking on the zoomed-up area to make it smaller.

Flipchart: *Special Flipchart p31*

Open the flipchart by clicking on the circled area and then on the Special Flipchart button ⍟.

Because of the length, this exercise is on two pages ① and ②.

Ask students to think about how they spend their free time. Ask one student to choose one of the four places (restaurant, gym, theatre or nightclub) and to write in, using the pen tool ✎, an appropriate time on the clock face.

Model the sentence structure (I will meet ___ at _____o'clock at the _____) if necessary.

Close the flipchart by clicking X in the toolbar.

Return to the double spread by clicking on the zoomed-up area to make it smaller.

Click on ▷ to go to the next double spread.

Double Spread p32/33

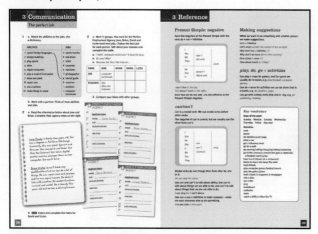

Flipchart: *Communication* **p32**
Open the flipchart by clicking on the circled area and then on .
1a Students work in pairs to match the abilities to the jobs in their books. Encourage students to use dictionaries and check in pairs.
Click on and ask a student to come to the interactive whiteboard to drag the jobs up and down in the column to the correct place next to the corresponding ability.

> **TIP:** *Drag temporarily unwanted jobs and 'park' on top of the lines to make room and avoid overwriting.*

To check the answers, click on to display the answers on a new page.
Click on to return to 1 to compare answers.

ANSWERS
1 g 2 i 3 a 4 b 5 j 6 h 7 c 8 e 9 f 10 d

> **TIP:** *For revision, now or later, on the answer page, click on* , *use a thick width and strong colour and ask a student to come to the interactive whiteboard and blank out all the jobs. Then students can see if they can remember them. Click on* *and erase the colour to reveal the jobs again. This can be done slowly to give students help with spelling or memory.*

Close the flipchart by clicking X in the toolbar.
Return to the double spread by clicking on the zoomed-up area to make it smaller.

Flipchart: *Communication* **p32**
Open the flipchart by clicking on the circled area and then on .
2a Elicit ways of looking for a job (ads in the paper, sending letters to companies, etc.) Explain what an employment agency is. Direct students to the Perfect Employment Agency notes for four people in their books. Make sure students understand *qualifications* (diploma; exams). Teach *a degree* and *notes* (pieces of important information, not full sentences).
Students read about Jane Danby and Brian Winter and complete the employment agency notes for them in their books. Check answers in pairs.
Click on and ask a student to come to the interactive whiteboard to write on the lines and complete the information for Jane and Brian.
To check the answers, click on to display the answers on a new page.
Click on to return to 1 to compare answers.

ANSWERS
Jane: 32; a degree in Art; can speak Spanish and German, can paint and draw, can take digital photos and change them on her computer; likes the Internet
Brian: 25; none; can repair cars and engines, can repair houses, can make furniture in wood and metal, can drive; doesn't like cold weather

Click on 2 .
b Click on so that students can listen to recording 3.11 and complete the information for the other two people in the notes in their books. Students check answers with a partner after the first listening. Click on to play the recording a second time. Click on and ask a student to come to the interactive whiteboard write on the lines and complete the information for David and Lizzie.
To check the answers, click on to display the answers on a new page.
Click on to return to 2 to compare answers.

ANSWERS
David: 22; certificate in computer programming; can play the piano and guitar, can drive; dislikes computer programming
Lizzie: 26, a college diploma in sports medicine; football, basketball, tennis, aerobics, dancing, can speak Portuguese; likes dancing

Close the flipchart by clicking X in the toolbar.
Return to the double spread by clicking on the zoomed-up area to make it smaller.
Click on the upwards pointing arrow to return to Unit 3, and then to return to the contents page to go to the next module.

Click on **page 35**. It will expand to fill the screen. Remember, you can zoom in to any part of the page by clicking on it, and return by clicking on it again.

Page 35

Flipchart: *Lead-in* **p35**

Open the flipchart by clicking on the circled area and then on AV.
2a Ask students to copy the table from their books into their notebooks. Students work with a partner to add all the food words they know under the correct column in their notebooks. Give them a time limit of three minutes for this to add an element of fun to the list making. See which pair has the longest list.
Click on ᒻ and ask a student to come to the interactive whiteboard to drag the words from the box into the correct columns. Click on [___] to display the answers in boxes below the columns.

> **ANSWERS:**
> beef, chicken, trout; butter cheese, milk; apples, cherries, watermelon; tea, water; bread, potatoes, rice, sugar, eggs

Then click on ✎ and ask students to come up to the interactive whiteboard and write in any more words they know to share with the rest of the group.
b In groups students talk about the different places they buy their food (supermarket, market, local shop, etc). Then they discuss how they pay (cash, cheque, credit card).

> **TIP:** *Use ✎ and ✐ in different colours to annotate the lists to show where students buy the food and pay for it. Change the colour by clicking on the coloured squares in the toolbar.*

Close the flipchart by clicking X in the toolbar.
Return to the double spread by clicking on the zoomed-up area to make it smaller.

Flipchart: *Your ideas* **p35**

Open the flipchart by clicking on the circled area and then on the Your Ideas button ✑.
Use this area to collate ideas from your students.
Use the pen tool ✎ to make notes on what students like to eat.
Use different colours for different student/groups. Then discuss

which column each item belongs in.
To follow up, discuss which food items would be eaten at which meal. Use the highlighter tool ✐ in three different colours to make the distinction.
Close the flipchart by clicking X in the toolbar.
Return to the double spread by clicking on the zoomed-up area to make it smaller.
Click on [>] to go to the next double spread.

Double Spread p36/37

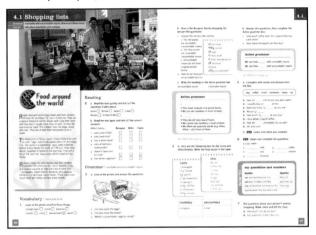

Flipchart: *Grammar* **p36**

Open the flipchart by clicking on the circled area and then on AV.
3a Focus students' attention on the picture on the interactive whiteboard. Students decide which of the items they can count (the eggs) and which they cannot (the cereal). Count the eggs with the students (1, 2, 3, 4 eggs). Click on ✎ (in the rubric or in the toolbar) and write the words *countable* and *uncountable* on the interactive whiteboard. Click on [___] to display the answers.

Optional Grammar lead-in: Students focus on the picture again. Ask: *What time of day is this?* (breakfast). Ask: *How do you know?* (eggs and Corn Flakes are typical breakfast food in English speaking countries). Ask: *What do you usually have for breakfast?* Elicit various suggestions, click on ✎ and write them on the interactive whiteboard. Put two headings either side of the picture on the interactive whiteboard, *countable* and *uncountable*. Ask students which column the suggestions should go under, e.g. coffee, bread, tea, orange juice, etc., for *uncountable*; biscuits, apples, etc., for *countable*. Try to elicit details about how many cups of coffee, how many pieces of toast, etc. Put x cups of coffee, 2 pieces of toast, etc., in the *countable* column.

b Click on [2]. Focus students' attention on the shopping list. In pairs, students decide whether the red and blue words are countable or uncountable and how they are measured.
Click on ✐ and ask a student to come to the interactive whiteboard to erase the incorrect words in the three sentences.

> **TIP:** *If students make a mistake, click on ↺ to undo the last action. You can also change the width of the eraser by dragging the slider below AV in the toolbar.*

Click on 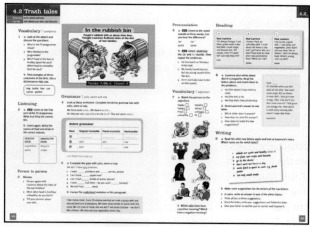 at the end of sentence 1 to highlight the answers.

ANSWERS:

1 a countable b uncountable c plural

Discuss 2 with the students and elicit the answer. Click on ✏ and write it on the line.
Click on ▭ at the end of sentence 2 to display the answer below the line.

ANSWERS:

2 use quantity words like litres or kilos in front of them.

Close the flipchart by clicking X in the toolbar.
Return to the double spread by clicking on the zoomed-up area to make it smaller.

Flipchart: *Grammar* **p37**

Open the flipchart by clicking on the circled area and then on ⒶⓋ.
4a This exercise is on ① and ②, with each shopping list on one page.
In pairs, students look at the two shopping lists in their books and decide whether the food words are countable or uncountable.
Click on ⬉ and ask a student to come to the interactive whiteboard to drag the words into the correct column.
Click on ▭ to display the answers in boxes below the columns.
Click on ② and repeat.

ANSWERS:

Costa family. Countable: pineapple, watermelons, papayas, bananas; Uncountable: bread, pasta, coffee, cereal; Ukita family. Countable: pizzas, eggs, tomatoes; Uncountable: rice, milk, tuna, beef, cola.

TIP: *Use ✏ to highlight the countable words in red and uncountable in blue.*

Click on ③.
b Students answer the two questions and complete the Active grammar box in their books. Check answers in pairs.
Click on ✏ and ask a student to come to the interactive whiteboard to write the answers to the questions along the lines provided.

Click on ▭ to display the answer below the lines.

ANSWERS:

1 500g of coffee 2 one pineapple many much

Direct students to the reference section on page 43.
Close the flipchart by clicking X in the toolbar.
Return to the double spread by clicking on the zoomed-up area to make it smaller.
Click on ▣ to go to the next double spread.

Double Spread p38/39

Flipchart: *Grammar* **p38**

Open the flipchart by clicking on the circled area and then on ⒶⓋ.
4 Students focus on the examples taken from the recording and complete the Active grammar box in their books in pairs.
Click on ✏ and ask a student to come to the interactive whiteboard to write the correct words on the lines in the Active grammar box.
Click on ▭ to display the answers below the lines.

ANSWERS:

a/an some some any

Refer students to the reference section on page 43.
Click on ②.
5a Students complete the exercise in their books in pairs.
Click on ✏ and ask a student to come to the interactive whiteboard to write the missing words on the lines in each sentence.
Click on ▭ to display the answers below the lines.

ANSWERS:

1 some / some 2 an 3 a 4 some / a 5 any

Click on ③.
b Students read the paragraph and correct the underlined mistakes in their books. Check answers in pairs.
Click on ✏ and ask a student to come to the interactive whiteboard to write the correct pair of words on the lines provided.
Click on ▭ to display the answers below the lines.

ANSWERS:

some pasta; some minced beef; some tomatoes; a bottle; any chicken; some vegetables.

TIP: *Click on ✏ and ask students to come to the interactive whiteboard and mark those countable and uncountable words with a big U (in blue) or C (in red).*

Close the flipchart by clicking X in the toolbar.
Return to the double spread by clicking on the zoomed-up area to make it smaller.

Flipchart: *Your ideas* **p38**

Open the flipchart by clicking on the circled area and then on the Your Ideas button ⁿ⌐.

Use this area to collate ideas from your students on what food they think is healthy and unhealthy. Remember, you can print these class notes directly from the screen.

Close the flipchart by clicking X in the toolbar.

Return to the double spread by clicking on the zoomed-up area to make it smaller.

Flipchart: *Pronunciation* **p39**

Open the flipchart by clicking on the circled area and then on ᴀᵥ̇.

6a Focus students' attention on the two words, *pasta* and *some*, on the interactive whiteboard. Click on 🔊 next to them on the left to play recording 4.4. Students listen to identify the two vowel sounds. Show the phonetic symbols for the two sounds.

> **TIP:** *You can move the audio window to a convenient place on the screen by clicking on the blue title bar and dragging the window to a clear space.*

> **TIP:** *If you want to repeat one of the words, just drag the slider back and then release.*

b Students read the sentences. Click on 🔊 (on the left of 6b) to play recording 4.5. Students listen and underline the /ae/ and /ʌ/ sounds in the sentences in their books.

Click on ✏ and ask a student to come to the interactive whiteboard. Ask them to choose a colour and highlight all the /ae/ sounds. Then click on a different coloured square in the toolbar to choose a different colour and highlight the /ʌ/ sounds.

Click on 🔲 to highlight the examples of both the sounds in the sentences.

> **ANSWERS:**
> /ae/1 He h<u>a</u>s lunch on Sundays in his club. 2 My f<u>a</u>mily tr<u>a</u>vels by t<u>a</u>xi, but my young cousin t<u>a</u>kes the bus.
> 3 <u>A</u>nne and S<u>a</u>lly have butter on their p<u>a</u>sta.
> /ʌ/1 He has l<u>u</u>nch on S<u>u</u>ndays in his cl<u>u</u>b. 2 My family travels by taxi, but my y<u>ou</u>ng c<u>ou</u>sin takes the b<u>u</u>s.
> 3 Anne and Sally have b<u>u</u>tter on their pasta.

Draw students' attention to the weak stress on *on* in connected speech. Refer students to the Pronunciation bank on page 148.

Close the flipchart by clicking X in the toolbar.

Return to the double spread by clicking on the zoomed-up area to make it smaller.

Flipchart: *Vocabulary* **p39**

Open the flipchart by clicking on the circled area and then on ᴀᵥ̇.

7a Students look at the pictures and match the pictures to the adjectives in their books. Check answers in pairs.

Click on ↳ and ask a student to come to the interactive whiteboard and drag the adjectives from the box in the middle onto the lines below the correct picture.

Click on 🔲 to display the answers in boxes below the lines.

> **ANSWERS:**
> A healthy B unhealthy C fit D tired E happy F unhappy G hungry H thirsty

Click on ② .

b Students categorise the adjectives in pairs.

Click on ↳ and ask a student to come to the interactive whiteboard and drag the adjectives from the box at the bottom into the correct column.

Click on 🔲 to display the answers in boxes on either side of the columns.

> **ANSWERS:**
> Positive: healthy, fit, happy Negative: unhealthy, tired, unhappy, hungry, thirsty

Close the flipchart by clicking X in the toolbar.

Return to the double spread by clicking on the zoomed-up area to make it smaller.

Click on ▣ to go to the next double spread.

Double Spread p40/41

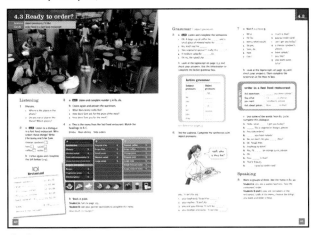

Flipchart: *Grammar* **p41**

Open the flipchart by clicking on the circled area and then on ᴀᵥ̇.

Click on 🔊 to play recording 4.8 once. Students listen to the extracts from the conversation in Ex. 5a and fill in the missing words in their books. Check answers in pairs.

> **TIP:** *If you want to give students a few seconds time to write after each sentence, just click on the slider in the audio window and hold for a few seconds and then release. This is quicker than clicking on pause and then play.*

Click on ✏ and ask a student to come to the interactive whiteboard to write the missing words on the lines to complete the sentences.

Click on 🔲 to display the answers in boxes below the lines.

> **ANSWERS:**
> 1 him / me 2 us 3 them 4 you 5 her

Alternatively, click on ▣ to view the tapescript and click on ✏ to highlight the missing words.

Click on ② .

b Students turn to the tapescript on page 153 and complete the Active grammar box in their books. Students check in pairs.

Click on ✏ and ask a student to come to the interactive whiteboard to write the missing object pronouns on the lines in the box.
Click on ✔ to display the answers at the side of the table.

ANSWERS:
me him her it us you them

Close the flipchart by clicking X in the toolbar.
Return to the double spread by clicking on the zoomed-up area to make it smaller.
Click on ▷ to go to the next double spread.

Double Spread p42/43

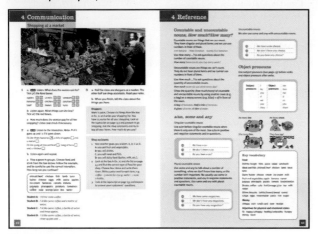

Flipchart: *Communication* **p42**
Focus students' attention on the picture of the market. Teach *stall* (a shop at a market)
Open the flipchart by clicking on the circled area and then on A∇.
1 Tell students they are going to hear a woman shopping at a market. Students look at the food words in their books. Click on 🔊 to play recording 4.9. Students tick the blue boxes in their books to show what the woman asked for and then check answers in pairs.
Click on ✏ and ask a student to come to the interactive whiteboard to tick the blue boxes.
Click on ✔ to display the answers in a box on the left below all the words.

ANSWERS:
1 She wants apples, bananas, melon from stall one; beef, tuna, chicken from stall two.

b Click on 🔊 to play recording 4.9. again. Students tick the red boxes in their books to show what she can buy and then check answers in pairs.
Click on ✏ and ask a student to come to the interactive whiteboard to tick the red boxes.
Click on ✔ to display the answers in a box on the right below all the words.

ANSWERS:
1 She can buy bananas and apples from stall one; beef and a chicken from stall two.

c Click on 🔊 to listen again if necessary. Students check in pairs.
Click on ✏ and ask a student to come to the interactive whiteboard to write the amount on the line.

Click on ✔ to display the amount below the line.

ANSWER:
18.50 euros

Close the flipchart by clicking X in the toolbar.
Return to the double spread by clicking on the zoomed-up area to make it smaller.

Flipchart: *Special flipchart* **p45**
Open the flipchart by clicking on the circled area and then on the Special Flipchart button 🖼.
Ask students to come to the whiteboard and choose some of the food on the left of the page. Select the ☞ tool and drag the pictures into the box. Ask the student to talk about what they chose, why they chose it and how much it would cost.

TIP: *If the food the student requires is not pictured, ask them to use the pen tool ✏ to write it into the box instead.*

Close the flipchart by clicking X in the toolbar.
Return to the double spread by clicking on the zoomed-up area to make it smaller.
Click on the upwards pointing arrow ⌂ to return to Unit 4, and then ⊞ to return to the contents page to go to the next module.

Click on **page 45**. It will expand to fill the screen. Remember, you can zoom in to any part of the page by clicking on it, and return by clicking on it again.

Page 45

Flipchart: *Lead-in* **p45**

Open the flipchart by clicking on the circled area and then on AV. Students look at the photos to identify the different rooms.

Click on ⬚ and ask a student to come to the interactive whiteboard to label the rooms correctly by dragging the words from the box onto the lines below each picture.

Click on ⬚ to display the answers in boxes at the top of each picture.

> **ANSWERS:**
> A bedroom B bathroom C living room D kitchen

Click on **2**.

b In their books, students look at the places in the box and match them to the activities. The first one is done for them. Students check answers in pairs.

Click on ⬚ and listen to recording 5.1.

> **TIP:** *Drag the audio window to the side.*

Click on ⬚ and ask a student to come to the interactive whiteboard and drag the names of the rooms up and down until they correspond to the correct activity.

Click on ⬚ to display the correct places on the right of the table.

> **ANSWERS:**
> 1 You can cook in the kitchen. 2 You can sleep in the bedroom. 3 You can have a shower in the bathroom.
> 4 You can put your car in the garage. 5 You can eat in the dining room/kitchen. 6 You can watch TV in the living room.

Ask students to use the prompts on the interactive whiteboard to say the complete sentences.

Close the flipchart by clicking X in the toolbar.

Return to the double spread by clicking on the zoomed-up area to make it smaller.

Flipchart: *Special Flipchart* **p45**

Open the flipchart by clicking on the circled area and then on the Special Flipchart button AV .

Because of the length, this exercise is on two pages **1** and **2**

Ask students to look at either the map of the U.K on page **1** or the map of the U.S on page **2** and think about where places shown are in relation to one another. E.g. Scotland is North of England. Model the sentence on the flipchart if you need to.

Ask students to describe the location of places to their partners.

Close the flipchart by clicking X in the toolbar.

Return to the double spread by clicking on the zoomed-up area to make it smaller.

Click on ⬚ to go to the next double spread.

Double Spread p46/47

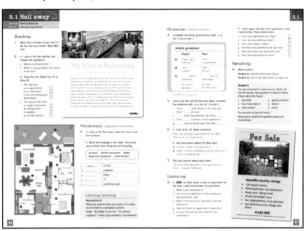

Flipchart: *Your Ideas* **p46**

Open the flipchart by clicking on the circled area and then on the Your Ideas button AV .

This blank flipchart is to record your students' discussions about their homes. Ask them to work in small groups and talk about the rooms in their house. Use the pen tool ✎ in a variety of colours to make notes on the interactive whiteboard.

Close the flipchart by clicking X in the toolbar.

Return to the double spread by clicking on the zoomed-up area to make it smaller.

Flipchart: *Vocabulary* **p46**

Open the flipchart by clicking on the circled area and then on AV.

3b Students work in pairs. They put the headings in the correct place in the table in their books and add two or three examples to each heading. Teach *facilities* (buildings and services near where you live – e.g. supermarket, library, playgrounds, etc.). Explain the difference between *furniture* and *equipment*.

Click on ⬚ and ask a student to come to the interactive whiteboard to drag the headings from the box at the top onto the lines next to each example. Click on ✎ and ask a student to come to the interactive whiteboard to write examples on the lines next to each heading.

Click on ⬚ to display the answers in boxes below the lines.

ANSWERS:

1 rooms (also living room, bathroom, etc.) 2 furniture (also bed, table, etc.) 3 kitchen equipment (also cooker, dishwasher, etc.). Note: People in Britain often have their washing machines in the kitchen. 4 living room equipment (also DVD, CD player, etc.) 5 ship's facilities (also gym, restaurants, etc.)

Close the flipchart by clicking X in the toolbar.
Return to the double spread by clicking on the zoomed-up area to make it smaller.

Flipchart: *Listening* **p47**
Tell students they are going to listen to a conversation between Jon and an estate agent for ResidenSea apartments. Elicit some examples of the kind of questions Jon might ask (*How much is it? How big is it? How many bedrooms are there?* etc.).
Open the flipchart.
8a Students look at the questions in their books. Click on 🔘 to play recording 5.3 once. Students listen and answer the questions. Check answers in pairs.
Click on ✎ and ask a student to come to the interactive whiteboard to write the answers on the lines after each question.

TIP: *When the student is at the interactive whiteboard, tell him to ask another class member the question, and then she can dictate the answer to him.*

You can either check each question as you work through by clicking on the small individual [answer]s at the end of each question or check all the questions together at the end by clicking on the larger [answer] at the bottom.
Click on [answer] to display the answers in boxes below the lines.

ANSWERS:

1 an apartment on The World of ResidenSea 2 two bedroom apartments only 3 two million dollars 4 Yes 5 Possibly, he says he will think about it. But maybe he doesn't want to say it is too expensive for him.

Click on [2] .
b Click on 🔘 and play the recording again. In their books, students number Jon's questions in the correct order and then answer them. Check answers in pairs. Click on ↖ and ask a student to come to the interactive whiteboard to drag the questions up and down to put them in the correct order. Click on ✎ and write the answers on the lines provided next to each question.
Click on [answer] to display the answers on a new page.

ANSWERS:

2 (Yes, of course); 4 (There are three two-bedroom apartments for sale); 6 (two and three bedrooms); 1 (2 bathrooms); 3 (100 sq metres and 120 sq metres) 5 (2 million dollars)

Click on 🔲 to return to [2] to compare your answers.

TIP: *For practice with the questions, on the Answer page, click on* 🔳 *in the toolbar, click on the right of the cover and drag it to the left so that the students can see only the answers. Elicit the questions from the students and then drag the cover further to the left to check. Click* 🔳 *again in the toolbar to remove the cover.*

Close the flipchart by clicking X in the toolbar.
Return to the double spread by clicking on the zoomed-up area to make it smaller.
Click on ⏩ to go to the next double spread.

Double Spread p48/49

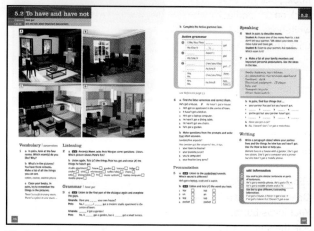

Flipchart: *Listening* **p48**
Open the flipchart by clicking on the circled area and then on AV.
2a Click on 🔘 to play recording 5.4 once. Students listen and decide which of the four photos is being described. Check answers in pairs. Click on ✎ and ask a student to come to the interactive whiteboard and tick the correct picture.
Click on [answer] to display the answer next to the box.

ANSWER:
C

Click on [2]
b Click on 🔘 to play the recording again. Students listen and, in their books, tick the items which Pete has got in his flat and cross the things he hasn't got. Check answers in pairs.
Click on ✎, click on the green coloured square to choose green, and ask a student to come to the interactive whiteboard to highlight the things Pete has got.
Click on the red coloured square to choose red, and ask a student to come to the interactive whiteboard to highlight the things Pete hasn't got. Click on [answer] to highlight the answers in the appropriate colours.

ANSWERS:

HAS GOT: studio apartment, terrace, fridge, cooker, sink, chairs, coffee table, sofa, TV, music system, laptop computer, mobile phone, dining table; HASN'T GOT: house, garden, microwave, dining table;

Close the flipchart by clicking X in the toolbar.
Return to the double spread by clicking on the zoomed-up area to make it smaller.

Flipchart: *Pronunciation* **p49**

Open the flipchart by clicking on the circled area and then on AV .
5a Click on ◉ on the left of the first sentence to play recording 5.6 once. Students listen and decide which sound is different. Check answers in pairs. Click on ✎ and ask a student to come to the interactive whiteboard and highlight the different sound. Click on ▒▒▒ at the end of the sentence to highlight the word with the different sound.

ANSWER:
c**a**t

b Click on ◉ to play recording 5.7. Students listen and, in their books, tick the words they hear. Check answers in pairs.
Click on ✎ and ask a student to come to the interactive whiteboard to tick the word they heard.
Click on ▒▒▒ to highlight answers.

ANSWERS:
1 hot 2 an 3 top 4 pocket

Close the flipchart by clicking X in the toolbar.
Return to the double spread by clicking on the zoomed-up area to make it smaller.

Flipchart: *Your Ideas* **p49**

Open the flipchart by clicking on the circled area and then on the Your Ideas button AV . .
Ask the students to look at the list (either on screen or in their books) and write down their own answers. Then click on ✎ ask a student to come up to the interactive whiteboard and share their ideas with the class.
Close the flipchart by clicking X in the toolbar.
Return to the double spread by clicking on the zoomed-up area to make it smaller.
Click on ▷ to go to the next double spread.

Double Spread p50/51

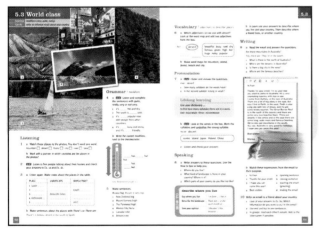

Flipchart: *Grammar* **p50**

Open the flipchart by clicking on the circled area and then on AV .
Ask students to look at the four sentences on the interactive whiteboard. See if they remember which place they refer to. (1 = the desert; 2 = Argentina; 3 = Poland; 4 = Osaka).
Click on ◉ to play recording 5.9. Students listen and complete the sentences in their books with the correct word.
Click on ✎ and ask a student to come to the interactive

whiteboard to write the correct word on the lines. You can either click on ▒▒▒ at the ends of each line to check answers consecutively, or click on ▒▒▒ at the bottom to check all the answers together.
Clicking on ▒▒▒ will display the answers below the lines.

ANSWERS:
1 really 2 very 3 quite 4 very / not very

Ask: *Which is the strongest?* (really and very); *Which is the weakest?* (not very). Click on ✎ to highlight the fact that the modifiers go before the adjective.
Click on 2 .
b Students look at the different thermometer readings and complete the scale in their books. Check answers in pairs.
Click on ✎ and ask a student to come to the interactive whiteboard to write the correct modifiers on the lines.
Click on ▒▒▒ to display the answers in boxes at the end of the lines.

ANSWERS:
40° = really hot, very hot 30° = hot 25° = quite hot
15° = not very hot

Direct students to the Reference page on page 53.
Close the flipchart by clicking X in the toolbar.
Return to the double spread by clicking on the zoomed-up area to make it smaller.

Flipchart: *Vocabulary* **p51**

Open the flipchart by clicking on the circled area and then on AV .
In their books, students add two further adjectives from the box to describe a desert. Students check in pairs. Click on ⌐ and ask a student to come to the interactive whiteboard to drag two adjectives from the box onto the lines.
Click on ▒▒▒ to display the answers in boxes below the lines.

ANSWERS:
dry famous

Click on 2 . There are three word maps on 2 and two on 3 .
b Students make word maps for the other nouns using adjectives from the box. There will be some overlap. Students compare in pairs.
Click on ✎ and ask a student to come to the interactive whiteboard and write suitable words to complete the word maps.
Click on 3 and repeat to complete the last two word maps.
Click on ▒▒▒ to display the answers on a new page.
Click on ◁ to return to 2 or 3 to compare your answers.

POSSIBLE ANSWERS:
mountain – beautiful, famous, high; island – beautiful, famous, noisy, huge, green, popular; forest – beautiful, green, huge, famous beach – beautiful, busy, famous, noisy, popular; city – beautiful, busy, famous, huge, noisy

Close the flipchart by clicking X in the toolbar.
Return to the double spread by clicking on the zoomed-up area to make it smaller.
Click on ▷ to go to the next double spread.

Double Spread p52/53

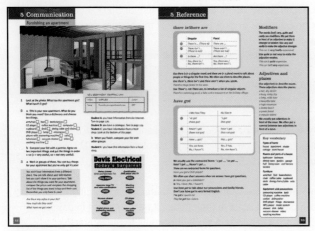

Flipchart: *Communication* **p52**

Open the flipchart by clicking on the circled area and then on AV.
Focus students' attention on the picture on the interactive whiteboard. Ask: *Do you like this apartment? Why/Why not?*
Students discuss with a partner what the apartment has and has not got. Click on ✏ and ask a student to come to the interactive whiteboard to label the things in the apartment. (cupboards, sink, fridge, cooker. Establish that there are no light fittings.)
Click on 2 .

2a Students look at the list of items in their books and choose ten things that they need to furnish the apartment. Students should use their dictionaries to look up words they don't know.
b Students work in pairs and compare their lists. Together they agree on ten items and rank them in order of importance with reasons. (E.g. I think a bed is very important. You have to sleep at night. You can sit on a bed but you can't sleep in a chair, etc.)
Don't worry about students making mistakes during this activity. Encourage students to express their opinions as best they can. Students compare lists with a different pair.

Click on 🔍 and ask a student to come to the interactive whiteboard to drag items from the left to a place on the right. It's easy to move any words if students change their minds. Try for a consensus among the students and ask them to justify their choices.

Close the flipchart by clicking X in the toolbar.
Return to the double spread by clicking on the zoomed-up area to make it smaller.

Click on the upwards pointing arrow ⬆ to return to Unit 5, and then ⬆ to return to the contents page to go to the next module.

Click on **page 55**. It will expand to fill the screen. Remember, you can zoom in to any part of the page by clicking on it, and return by clicking on it again.

Page 55

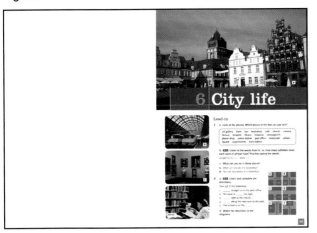

Flipchart: *Your Ideas* **p55**

Open the flipchart by clicking on the circled area and then on the Your Ideas button .

Use this flipchart for a brainstorming session on the buildings in the city in which you live (or the city closest to where you live) .

Use the pen tool to write or even draw your ideas onto the interactive whiteboard.

Use the eraser tool if any mistakes are made.

Close the flipchart by clicking X in the toolbar.

Return to the double spread by clicking on the zoomed-up area to make it smaller.

Flipchart: *Lead-in* **p55**

Open the flipchart by clicking on the circled area and then on AV .

2a Click on to play recording 6.2. Students listen and complete the directions in their books with the missing word. Click on and ask a student to come to the interactive whiteboard to write the words on the lines to complete the directions.

Click on on the left to display the answers for 2a only in boxes below the lines.

> **ANSWERS:**
> left 1 Go 2 on 3 Turn 4 Go 5 left

b In their books, students match the directions to the diagrams. Check answers in pairs. Click on and ask a student to come to the interactive whiteboard and write the letter of the corresponding diagram in the box at the end of the sentence. Click on to display the letters next to the boxes.

> **ANSWERS:**
> Example B; 1 F; 2 C; 3 A; 4 E; 5 D

> **TIP:** *For further practice, click on and drag the cover to the left, so that only the diagrams are showing. Ask students if they can remember the directions for each diagram. Click on to listen to the recording again to check.*

Close the flipchart by clicking X in the toolbar.

Return to the double spread by clicking on the zoomed-up area to make it smaller.

Click on to go to the next double spread.

Double Spread p56/57

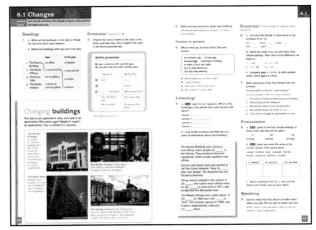

Flipchart: *Grammar* **p56**

Open the flipchart by clicking on the circled area and then on AV .

2 Students look at the four texts in their books again. Ask students to underline all the verbs in the sentences in their books. (All the verbs are *is/are* and *was/were*.)

Students choose the correct words in the rules and then complete the Active grammar box in their books and check answers in pairs.

Click on and ask a student to come to the interactive whiteboard and erase the incorrect words in the rules. Click on and ask another student to come to the interactive whiteboard and write the correct words on the lines to complete the Active grammar box.

Click on to highlight the correct choices and display the missing words in boxes on the right.

> **ANSWERS:**
> now the past. were wasn't Was wasn't were

Help students with the initial /w/ sound in *was* and *were* and the weak vowel sound /ə/ in affirmative and negative sentences. Click on and highlight the contracted negative form.

Close the flipchart by clicking X in the toolbar.

Return to the double spread by clicking on the zoomed-up area to make it smaller.

Flipchart: *Pronunciation* **p57**

Open the flipchart by clicking on the circled area and then on AV .

8a Click on to play recording 6.4. Click on and ask: are the sounds all the same? Write *no* on the interactive whiteboard. Students repeat the verbs and practise the sounds. Click on 2 .

b Click on to play recording 6.5 and students write the verbs in the correct column in their books.

Click on and ask a student to come to the interactive whiteboard to drag the verbs from the box at the top into the correct column.

Click on [icon] to display the answers in boxes below the columns.

> **ANSWERS:**
> /t/: finished, looked, produced
> /d/: lived, changed, planned, studied
> /ɪd/: visited, started

Say: *finished.* Ask: *How many syllables do you hear?* (two, not three syllables). Say: *looked, changed.* Ask: *How many syllables do you hear?* (one, not two) Ask: *When does the past tense ending sound like a new syllable /d/?* (After verbs ending in /t/ and /d/.)

> **TIP:** Use ✎ to highlight the /ɪd/ ending.

c Students practise reading sentences from Ex. 7 in pairs. Students correct each other. Monitor closely, refer to the interactive whiteboard and correct any mis-pronunciation of past tense endings.
Close the flipchart by clicking X in the toolbar.
Return to the double spread by clicking on the zoomed-up area to make it smaller.
Click on [icon] to go to the next double spread.

Double Spread p58/59

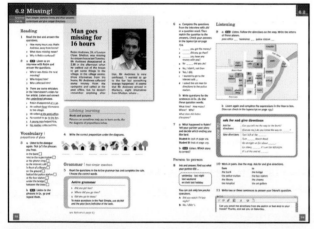

Flipchart: *Vocabulary* p58

Open the flipchart by clicking on the circled area and then on AV.
This exercise is on two pages 1 and 2.
In their books, students write the correct preposition under each diagram and check in pairs.
Click on ✎ and ask a student to come to the interactive whiteboard and write the correct preposition under each diagram. You can click on 2 and finish the exercise and then return to 1 to check each page, or check 1 before continuing with 2.
Click on [icon] to display the answers below the lines.

> **ANSWERS:**
> in   next to   in front of   behind   under   on   between

Close the flipchart by clicking X in the toolbar.
Return to the double spread by clicking on the zoomed-up area to make it smaller.

Flipchart: *Grammar* p59

Open the flipchart by clicking on the circled area and then on AV.
6a In their books, students complete the questions, then match the questions to the answers a–d. Students check answers in pairs.
Click on ✎ and ask a student to come to the interactive whiteboard to write on the lines to complete the questions. Click on [icon] on the left to display the answers above the lines.
Click on ↖ and ask a student to come to the interactive whiteboard to drag the answers up and down on the right to correspond to the correct questions.
Click on [icon] on the right to display the answers in boxes on the right.

> **ANSWERS:**
> 1 Did b   2 Where c   3 Did a   4 what d

> **TIP:** Use the cover sheet to hide the answers. Click on [icon] and drag the cover to the right to show the questions. See if students can remember the answers and then drag the cover to the right to reveal them.

Close the flipchart by clicking X in the toolbar.
Return to the double spread by clicking on the zoomed-up area to make it smaller.

Flipchart: *Special Flipchart* p59

Open the flipchart by clicking on the circled area and then on the Special Flipchart button [icon].
Ask students to look at the three pictures on 1 and formulate *yes/no* questions using Did you _____ last weekend?
Put the class into pairs to practice saying the first three sentences, then click on 2 to see the next three.
Close the flipchart by clicking X in the toolbar.
Return to the double spread by clicking on the zoomed-up area to make it smaller.
Click on [icon] to go to the next double spread.

Double Spread p60/61

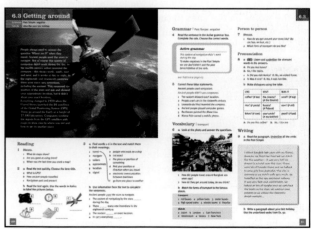

Flipchart: *Reading* p60

Open the flipchart by clicking on the circled area and then on AV.
3a Students look at the text in their books again. They find the words 1–6 in the text and try to guess what these words mean before matching them to the six meanings given. The first one is done for them. Students check answers in pairs.

Click on 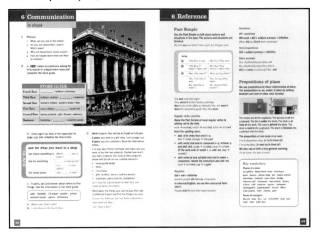 and ask a student to come to the interactive whiteboard and drag the meanings on the right up and down to correspond with the words.
Click on ⬚⬚⬚ to display the answers in boxes on the right.

> **ANSWERS:**
> 1/f 2/d 3/a 4/b 5/c 6/e

> **TIP:** *For further practice, click on ✎, drag the slider to increase the width and using red (for example) ask a student to come to the interactive whiteboard and blank out all the vocabulary on the left. Then students can see if they can remember the words from the meanings. Check spelling too. Click on ✎ and erase the red to reveal the words again. This can be done slowly to give students clues if they are having difficulty remembering.*

Close the flipchart by clicking X in the toolbar.
Return to the double spread by clicking on the zoomed-up area to make it smaller.

Flipchart: *Vocabulary* **p61**

Open the flipchart by clicking on the circled area and then on A⋁.
Ask students: *How do people get to work every day today?* (car, bus, walk, etc.) and *How did people get to work 100 years ago?* (walk, bicycle, etc.) Elicit the other ways of getting around. Teach *by car/bicycle/train/taxi/tram/boat/plane* but *on foot*.
Students look at the photo on the interactive whiteboard and discuss the answers to the two questions. Click on ✎ and ask a student to come to the interactive whiteboard to write the answers on the lines.
Click on ⬚⬚⬚ to display the answers below the lines.

> **ANSWERS:**
> 1 by boat 2 By car/by bus/by boat/by taxi

Click on 2 .
b In their books, students match the forms of transport to the places. Students check in pairs. Click on ⬚ and ask a student to come to the interactive whiteboard to drag the places on the right up and down to correspond to the form of transport.
Click on ⬚⬚⬚ to display the answers in boxes on the right.

> **ANSWERS:**
> 1/b 2/f 3/e 4/a 5/c 6/d

Find out if students have visited any of these cities and elicit if they used any of the forms of transport mentioned.
Close the flipchart by clicking X in the toolbar.
Return to the double spread by clicking on the zoomed-up area to make it smaller.

Flipchart: *Your Ideas* **p61**

Open the flipchart by clicking on the circled area and then on the Your Ideas button ⬚.
Use this flipchart to put together some notes on the forms of transport used by your students. Ask them to describe when they use it/where they go/whether it is fast, cheap, etc.
Close the flipchart by clicking X in the toolbar.
Return to the double spread by clicking on the zoomed-up area to make it smaller.

Double Spread p62/63

Flipchart: *Communication* **p62**

Open the flipchart by clicking on the circled area and then on A⋁.
2a Teach *escalator* (moving stairs), *on the ground/first/second floor* and *in the basement*. Click on ⬚ to play recording 6.11 and students complete the gaps in the Store Guide in their books. Check answers in pairs. Click on ✎ and ask a student to come to the interactive whiteboard to write on the lines to complete the guide.
Click on ⬚⬚⬚ to display the answers in boxes below the lines.

> **ANSWERS:**
> furniture / music / men' shoes / computers

Click on 2 .
b Click on ⬚ to play the recording again and students complete the How to box in their books. Check answers in pairs. Click on ✎ and ask a student to come to the interactive whiteboard to write on the lines to complete the questions.
Click on ⬚⬚⬚ to display the answers in boxes below the lines.

> **ANSWERS:**
> can I find / Have you got / I have / much

> **TIP:** *Use ⬚ to cover the right side and try to elicit the questions from the group. Ask for suggestions of things to ask for from other students.*

Close the flipchart by clicking X in the toolbar.
Return to the double spread by clicking on the zoomed-up area to make it smaller.
Click on the upwards pointing arrow ⬚ to return to Unit 6, and then on ⬚⬚⬚ to return to the contents page to go to the next module.

Flipchart: *Your Ideas* **p65**
Open the flipchart by clicking on the circled area and then on the
Your Ideas button 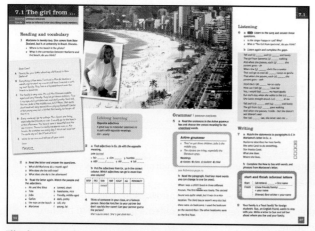.
Using the pen tool ✏ make notes on vocabulary that can be used
to describe appearance. Ask a volunteer to talk about themself,
using the flipchart notes to help them.
Close the flipchart by clicking X in the toolbar.
Return to the page by clicking on the zoomed-up area to make it
smaller.

Click on ⧉ to go to the next double spread.
Click on the **double spread p66/67**. It will expand to fill the
screen. Remember, you can zoom in to any part of the page by
clicking on it, and return by clicking on it again.

Flipchart: *Special flipchart* **p65**
Open the flipchart by clicking on the circled area and then on the
Special Flipchart button.
Use the pictures of the people over the 3 pages to prompt
discussion about the way people look. Put the students into small
groups and ask them to talk about either picture on page 1. Ask
them to come up to the whiteboard and describe their picture,
using the pen tool ✏ to annotate the picture as they talk.
Move on to pages 2 and 3 and repeat the exercise.

Close the flipchart by clicking X in the toolbar.
Return to the page by clicking on the zoomed-up area to make it
smaller.

Double Spread p66/67

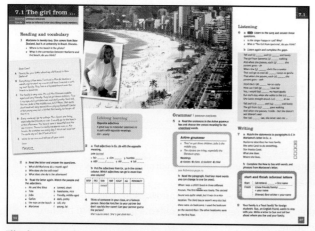

Flipchart: *Reading and Vocabulary* **p66**
Open the flipchart by clicking on the circled area and then on AV.
3a In their books, students look at the adjectives in exercise 2b
again and match them to their opposites. Students check in pairs.
Click on ✏ and ask a student to come to the interactive
whiteboard to write the opposite adjectives on the lines.
Click on to display the answers in boxes at the ends of the
lines.

ANSWERS:
1 dark 2 fat 3 nice 4 handsome/pretty 5 young 6 short

Click on 2
b In pairs, students write the adjectives into the correct columns
in their books.
Click on ⬆ and ask a student to come to the interactive
whiteboard and drag each adjective into an appropriate column.
There are 7 copies of each adjective so students can repeat an
adjective as often as they want.
Click on to display the answers below the columns.

ANSWERS:
Body: slim, fat; Face: pretty, handsome, ugly; Skin:
tanned, pale, fair, dark; Hair fair, dark; Height: tall,
short; Age: old, middle-aged, young; Personality: shy,
nice; *Fair* and *dark* can be used to describe both hair and
skin colour. *Nice* and *horrible* can be used to describe
body, face, skin, hair, and personality.

TIP: *Click on* ✏ *to highlight the adjectives that can be used in
more than one column.*

Close the flipchart by clicking X in the toolbar.
Return to the double spread by clicking on the zoomed-up area to
make it smaller.

Flipchart: *Grammar* **p67**
Open the flipchart by clicking on the circled area and then on AV.
5a Students look at the two sentences in the Active grammar box
on the interactive whiteboard and find them in the letter they read
in their books (on p66). Ask students to match the underlined
words to their meanings below and check in pairs. Click on ⬆ and
ask a student to come to the interactive whiteboard to drag the
correct meaning onto the line.
Click on to display the answers in boxes at the end of the
lines.

ANSWERS:
1 child 2 classes

One replaces singular nouns, *ones* replaces plural nouns. We
often use *one* and *ones* to replace the noun after an adjective or
after *this/these* and *that/those*. We also use *one* after *each*
(Students will hear this in the song in Ex. 6a) and in expressions
like *the one/ones on the left/right*, etc. Direct students to the
reference section on page 73.
Click on 2 .

b Students read the paragraph in their books and find four words
which could be replaced by *one* or *ones*. Students check answers
in pairs.
Click on ✏ and ask a student to come to the interactive
whiteboard to change four words into *one* or *ones*.
Click on to display the answers on a new page.
Click on ⌂ to return to 2 to compare your answers.

ANSWERS:
The second one; The third one; the one on the second
floor; The other ones

Close the flipchart by clicking X in the toolbar.
Return to the double spread by clicking on the zoomed-up area to make it smaller.

Flipchart: *Listening* **p67**
Open the flipchart by clicking on the circled area and then on [A∨].
6a Students look at the two questions on the interactive whiteboard. Students listen to the song on the Class CD and answer the questions in their books. Students check in pairs. Click on / and ask a student to come to the interactive whiteboard to write the answers on the lines.

> **ANSWERS:**
> 1 sad because the girl does not notice him. 2 Students' own answers

Click on [2]. The song is on two pages [2] and [3].
b Students look at the words of the song. Teach *samba* (a type of dance) and *pause* (stop for a moment). Review *straight ahead* from the previous unit. Use ✐ to highlight these words. Students read through the song in their books and try to guess what the missing words might be. Students compare answers in pairs. Students listen and fill in the missing words in their books. Students check answers in pairs.
Click on / and ask a student to come to the interactive whiteboard to write the missing words on the lines provided. Click on [3] and complete the song before clicking on [2] to check from the beginning.
Click on [✓✓] to display the answers for each page in boxes below the lines.

> **ANSWERS:**
> 1 tanned 2 young 3 goes 4 one 5 walks 6 and 7 one
> 8 watch 9 her 10 give 11 sea 12 not 13 tanned 14 young
> 15 Ipanema 16 doesn't

> **TIP:** *Students often enjoy singing along to the song to finish off the activity. It's much more effective to do this when they can all look up at the interactive whiteboard to read the lyrics.*

Close the flipchart by clicking X in the toolbar.
Return to the double spread by clicking on the zoomed-up area to make it smaller.
Click on [»] to go to the next double spread.

Double Spread p68/69

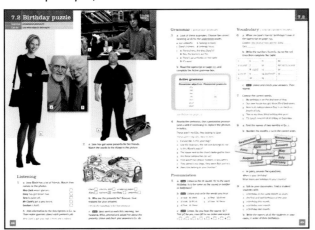

Flipchart: *Listening* **p68**
Open the flipchart by clicking on the circled area and then on [A∨].
1a Students look at the photos of Jane's friends on the interactive whiteboard. Click on ▦ and drag the cover to the left to hide the sentences. In pairs, they describe each person in the photos without looking at the sentences in their books (e.g. hair colour, height, etc.). Students look at their books and match the descriptions to the photos. Students check answers in pairs. Click on ▦ in the toolbar to remove the cover. Click on / and ask a student to come to the interactive whiteboard and write the number of the picture in the box next to the correct sentence. Click on [✓✓] to display the answers in boxes next to the boxes at the end of the descriptions.

> **ANSWERS:**
> Mrs Clark 3; Davy 1; Tara 5; Mr Clark 2; Gordon 4

Click on [2].
b Elicit more information to describe the five people. Students make guesses about what their jobs might be. An example is given in the book. Click on / and ask a student to come to the interactive whiteboard and write on the lines to add to the description. Discuss with the class.
Close the flipchart by clicking X in the toolbar.
Return to the double spread by clicking on the zoomed-up area to make it smaller.

Flipchart: *Pronunciation* **p69**
Open the flipchart by clicking on the circled area and then on [A∨].
5a Focus students' attention on *brother* and *bathroom* on the interactive whiteboard. Click on ✐ and highlight the *th* in both words. Say the two words. Ask: *Is the 'th' sound the same?* (No, *brother* is /ð/ and *bathroom* is /θ/). Click on / and write the two phonetic symbols on the interactive whiteboard.
Look at *birthday* on the interactive whiteboard. Do not pronounce it yet. Ask: *Which sound is in this word?* Click on 🔊 on the left of 5a to play recording 7.4. Students listen and identify the /θ/ sound.
Students practise saying the words *birthday* and *bathroom*.
b Students look at the words. Click on 🔊 on the left of 5b to play recording 7.5. Students listen and circle the word they hear in their books. Check answers in pairs. Click on ✐ and ask a student to come to the interactive whiteboard and highlight the words they heard.
Click on [✓✓] to highlight the answers.

> **ANSWERS:**
> 1 b thick 2 b think 3 a free 4 b thirst 5 b three

Click on [2].
c Click on 🔊 above button to play recording 7.6. Students listen and tick or cross the numbers in their books. Click on / and ask a student to come to the interactive whiteboard and write a tick against the number of the words with /θ/ that they heard.
Click on [✓✓] to display the answers next to the boxes.

> **ANSWERS:**
> 1 (✓) 2 (✓) 3 (✗) 4 (✗) 5 (✓) 6 (✓) 7 (✗) 8 (✓)

Close the flipchart by clicking X in the toolbar.
Return to the double spread by clicking on the zoomed-up area to make it smaller.

Flipchart: *Vocabulary* **p69**

Open the flipchart by clicking on the circled area and then on AV .
8b Students look at the jumbled months and put them in order in their books. January has been numbered 1 for them. Students check in pairs. Click on ✏ and ask a student to come to the interactive whiteboard to write the numbers next to the months. Click on ▭ to display the answers in boxes next to the months.

> **ANSWERS:**
> January 1 February 2 March 3 April 4 May 5 June 6 July 7 August 8 September 9 October 10 November 11 December 12

Students practise saying the months.

> **TIP:** *For spelling practice, click on ✏, drag the slider to increase the width and using blue (for example) ask a student to come to the interactive whiteboard and blank out all the months. Then students can see if they can remember them. Click on ✐ and erase the blue to reveal the months again. This can be done slowly to give students help with the spelling.*

c Students tell their partner their birthdays and give the dates of national holidays in their country. Click on ✏ and ask a student to come to the interactive whiteboard to write their birthday and national holidays as an example. Check that students know how to write dates correctly.
Close the flipchart by clicking X in the toolbar.
Return to the double spread by clicking on the zoomed-up area to make it smaller.
Click on ▶ to go to the next double spread.

Double Spread p70/71

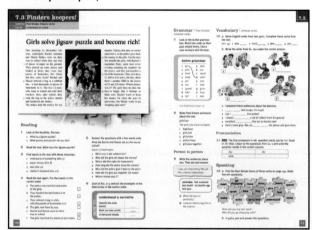

Flipchart: *Grammar* **p71**

Open the flipchart by clicking on the circled area and then on AV .
7 Ask students to look back at the Reading text and underline the verb in the first sentence *(were)*. They should be familiar with the past simple of the verb *to be*. Explain this is an irregular past tense. It has no *-ed* ending. Students look at more irregular verbs from the text in the Active grammar box. They match the present to the past forms of each verb in their books. Students check in pairs.
Click on ⬚ and ask a student to come to the interactive whiteboard to drag the past forms of the verbs on the right up and down to correspond with the correct verb.

Click on ▭ to display the answers on the right.

> **ANSWERS:**
> 1/d 2/g 3/i 4/h 5/b 6/e 7/c 8/a 9/f

> **TIP:** *Click on ▣ and drag the cover to the right to cover the past simple forms. See if students can remember them. Then click on ▣ to remove the cover and reveal them.*

Many of the most common verbs in English are irregular. They do not have an *-ed* ending.
Direct students to the reference section on page 73.
Close the flipchart by clicking X in the toolbar.
Return to the double spread by clicking on the zoomed-up area to make it smaller.

Flipchart: *Your Ideas* **p71**

Open the flipchart by clicking on the circled area and then on the Your Ideas button ✏▢ .
Put the class into groups and ask them to work together to create five questions, using five puzzle pieces to help. Then ask the groups to pair up and ask and answer their questions.
Close the flipchart by clicking X in the toolbar.
Return to the double spread by clicking on the zoomed-up area to make it smaller.
Click on ▶ to go to the next double spread.

Double Spread p72/73

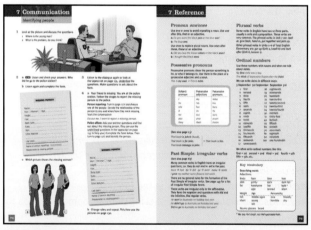

Flipchart: *Communication* **p72**

Open the flipchart by clicking on the circled area and then on AV .
1 Students focus on the picture on the interactive whiteboard. Discuss where the man in the picture is and why.
Click on ✏ and ask a student to come to the interactive whiteboard to write the answers.
Click on ▭ to display the answers below the lines.

> **ANSWERS:**
> 1 He is in a police station. 2 We don't know why.

Close the flipchart by clicking X in the toolbar.
Return to the double spread by clicking on the zoomed-up area to make it smaller.
Click on the upwards pointing arrow ▣ to return to Unit 7, and then on ▭ to return to the contents page to go to the next module.

Click on **page 75**. It will expand to fill the screen. Remember, you can zoom in to any part of the page by clicking on it, and return by clicking on it again.

Page 75

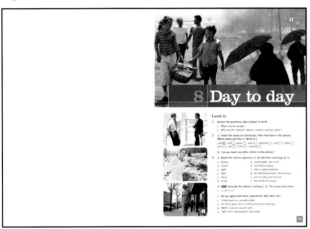

Flipchart: *Your Ideas* **p75**
Open the flipchart by clicking on the circled area and then on the Your Ideas button ⬚.
Use this area to collate ideas from your students.
Talk about the different seasons and what kind of weather we see in them. Then make some notes with the ✎ tool on everyone's favourite time of the year and what they like to do best.
Close the flipchart by clicking X in the toolbar.
Return to the page by clicking on the zoomed-up area to make it smaller.

> **ANSWERS:**
> 1 d 2 e 3 f 4 b 5 a 6 c

> **TIP:** *Use the cover sheet to hide the adjectives. Click on ▣ in the toolbar and drag the pointer to the left and reveal the meanings. See if students can remember the adjectives and then click on ▣ to remove the cover.*

Close the flipchart by clicking X in the toolbar.
Return to the page by clicking on the zoomed-up area to make it smaller.
Click on ⬙ to go to the next double spread.

Flipchart: *Lead-in* **p75**
Open the flipchart by clicking on the circled area and then on 🄰.
3a In their books, students match the adjectives to their meanings and check answers in pairs. Click on 🄺 and ask a student to come to the interactive whiteboard to drag the meanings up and down on the right to correspond with the words.
Click on ▨ to display the answers on the right.

Double Spread p76/77

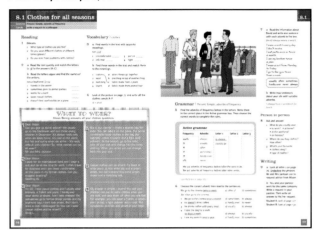

Flipchart: *Your Ideas* **p76**
Open the flipchart by clicking on the circled area and then on the Your Ideas button 🄰.
Use this area to collate ideas from your students.
Talk about the different kinds of clothes everyone likes to wear.
Then make some notes on the students' favourites with the ✎ tool.
Close the flipchart by clicking X in the toolbar.
Return to the double spread by clicking on the zoomed-up area to make it smaller.

Flipchart: *Vocabulary* **p76**
Open the flipchart by clicking on the circled area and then on 🄰.
Click on ✐ to draw students' attention to the prefixes *un-* and *in-* but do not spend too long on this.
3a Students focus on the vocabulary in the text in their books. They find words with opposite meanings to those listed. Students check answers in pairs.
Click on ✎ and ask a student to come to the interactive whiteboard and write the opposites.
Click on ▨ to display the answers below the lines.

> **ANSWERS:**
> 1 comfortable 2 formal 3 take off 4 loose

b Students match the four words from the text to their meanings in their books. The first one has been done for them. Students check answers in pairs.
Click on 🄺 and ask a student to come to the interactive whiteboard to drag the meanings on the right up and down to correspond to the words.
Click on ▨ to display the answers on the right of the table.

> **ANSWERS:**
> 1 c 2 d 3 a 4 b

Click on ✐ and focus on the pronunciation of these words (especially *wool* and *layers*), highlighting any difficult sounds for your students.
Close the flipchart by clicking X in the toolbar.
Return to the double spread by clicking on the zoomed-up area to make it smaller.

Flipchart: *Grammar* **p77**

Open the flipchart by clicking on the circled area and then on 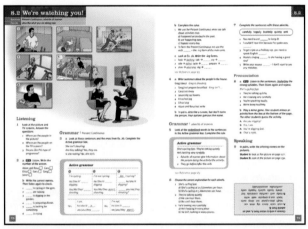 ⒶⓋ.

6 This exercise is on two pages ① and ② .

> **TIP:** *Click on ✐ to highlight the use of the indefinite article in once a week, six days a week etc.*

Students work in pairs. They choose the most appropriate adverb of frequency and rewrite the sentences in their books. The first one has been done for them.

Click on ✐ and ask a student to come to the interactive whiteboard to write the revised sentences on the lines.

Click on ⬚⬚⬚⬚ to highlight the correct adverb and display the corrected sentences below the lines.

> **ANSWERS:**
> 1 We <u>sometimes</u> go to the cinema 2 He <u>never</u> drinks coffee 3 He <u>always</u> drinks coffee 4 I <u>usually</u> take the dog for a walk 5 I <u>hardly ever</u> see my parents

Close the flipchart by clicking X in the toolbar.

Return to the double spread by clicking on the zoomed-up area to make it smaller.

Click on ⬚ to go to the next double spread.

Double Spread p78/79

Flipchart: *Listening* **p78**

Open the flipchart by clicking on the circled area and then on ⒶⓋ

2a Teach *to have an argument with someone* (to disagree with, shout at someone). Click on 🔊 to play recording 8.2. Students listen and match the name of the person to the TV screen picture. Students check answers in pairs.

Click on 🔾 and ask a student to come to the interactive whiteboard to drag the names from the middle onto the space below the corresponding screen.

Click on ⬚⬚⬚⬚ to display the answers on the bottom part of the screens.

> **ANSWERS:**
> 1 Greg 2 Cara 3 Jason 4 Erica 5 Adam and Rosa
> 6 Gary

Click on ② .

b Click on 🔊 to play the recording again. Students listen and complete the sentences with the correct name in their books. Students check answers in pairs. Click on 🔾 and ask a student to

come to the interactive whiteboard to drag the names from the box on the right onto the lines of the correct sentences.

Click on ⬚⬚⬚⬚ to display the answers below the lines.

> **ANSWERS:**
> 1 Erica 2 Adam and Rosa
> 3 Jason 4 Greg 5 Gary 6 Cara

Close the flipchart by clicking X in the toolbar.

Return to the double spread by clicking on the zoomed-up area to make it smaller.

Flipchart: *Pronunciation* **p79**

Open the flipchart by clicking on the circled area and then on ⒶⓋ.

8a Click on 🔊 to play recording 8.3. Students listen and, in their books, underline the strong syllables in the sentences they hear. The first one has been done for them.

> **TIP:** *If students need time to write, just click on the slider in the audio window and hold it for a few seconds and then release. This is quicker than using Pause. Also, if you want to repeat, just drag the slider back and then release.*

Students check answers in pairs. Click on ✐ and ask a student to come to the interactive whiteboard to underline the strong syllables.

Click on ⬚⬚⬚⬚ to display the answers below the sentences.

> **ANSWERS:**
> 1 They're <u>talking quietly</u>. 2 He's <u>looking</u> very <u>carefully</u>. 3 You're <u>speaking loudly</u>. 4 We're <u>living healthily</u>.

Click on 🔊 to listen again and ask students to repeat. Pause as necessary.

Click on ② .

b Students mime one of the verb and adverb combinations from the box and the other students try to guess the activity. Model an example first for students.

Click on ✐ and ask a student to come to the interactive whiteboard to highlight the verb and adverb chosen.

> **TIP:** *To make the game more challenging, click on ▦ and drag the cover to the left to hide the box of activities. Drag the cover to the left if students need to be reminded of the words and to highlight the students' choices, and then drag to cover again.*

Close the flipchart by clicking X in the toolbar.

Return to the double spread by clicking on the zoomed-up area to make it smaller.

Click on ⬚ to go to the next double spread.

Double Spread p80/81

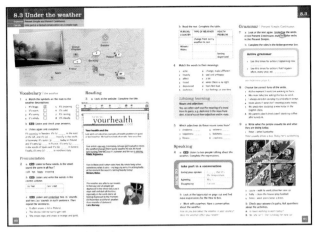

Flipchart: *Special Flipchart* p80

Open the flipchart by clicking on the circled area and then on the Special Flipchart button ⟨⟩.

This exercise is designed to encourage communication. Students should imagine that they are TV weathermen/women and that they need to talk about the weather. Using the ⟨⟩ tool, drag the symbols from the right side of the page onto the map.

Students can choose between the map of Europe on page ⟨1⟩ , the U.K on page ⟨2⟩ or the U.S on page ⟨3⟩ .

Close the flipchart by clicking X in the toolbar.

Return to the double spread by clicking on the zoomed-up area to make it smaller.

Flipchart: *Reading* p81

Open the flipchart by clicking on the circled area and then on ⟨AV⟩ .

4 Students focus on the new vocabulary in the text in their books. They match the words to the correct meaning and check answers in pairs. Click on ⟨⟩ and ask a student to come to the interactive whiteboard to drag the meanings on the right up and down to correspond to the words.

Click on ⟨⟩ to display the answers on the right.

> **ANSWERS:**
> 1 e 2 c 3 a 4 f 5 b 6 d

> **TIP:** *Click on* ⟨⟩ *, elicit the stress and mark it with a 'blob'. Remember you can change the width of the highlighter by dragging the slider on the toolbar. Drill pronunciation of these words.*

Close the flipchart by clicking X in the toolbar.

Return to the double spread by clicking on the zoomed-up area to make it smaller.

Flipchart: *Grammar* p81

Open the flipchart by clicking on the circled area and then on ⟨AV⟩ .

9a This exercise is on four pages, ⟨1⟩ , ⟨2⟩ , ⟨3⟩ , and ⟨4⟩ . Each picture is on a new page. Students write sentences in their books about the people in the pictures, using the prompts. The first one is done for them. Model this on the whiteboard. Students check answers in pairs.

Click on ⟨⟩ and ask a student to come to the interactive whiteboard to erase the box covering the prompt above the picture. Click on ⟨⟩ and write the sentence on the lines next to the picture. Click on ⟨2⟩ and repeat the erasing and writing for each

picture. You can either click on ⟨⟩ at the bottom of each page to check answers as you go along, or you can click on ⟨2⟩ , ⟨3⟩ and then ⟨4⟩ and finish the exercise and then return to ⟨1⟩ to check each page.

Clicking on ⟨⟩ will display the answers below the lines.

> **ANSWERS:**
> 1 Peter usually drives a bus. Today he's sunbathing.
> 2 Laura usually walks to work. Today she is driving her new car. 3 Sally usually cleans the house every day. Today she is playing football. 4 Anna usually wears jeans. Today she is wearing a dress.

You can use the pictures on each page for exercise b. Click on ⟨⟩ to annotate the pictures as you wish and students practise the two tenses by asking each other questions about the people in the pictures like the example given in their books.

Close the flipchart by clicking X in the toolbar.

Return to the double spread by clicking on the zoomed-up area to make it smaller.

Click on ⟨⟩ to go to the next double spread.

Double Spread p82/83

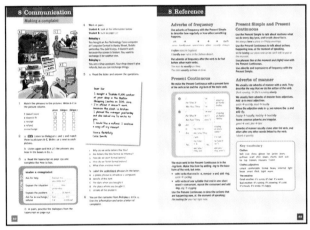

Flipchart: *Communication* p82

Open the flipchart by clicking on the circled area and then on ⟨AV⟩ .

3a Elicit the stages in making a complaint. *What do you do first/second?*, etc. (Explain the problem, ask for money/exchange, etc.). Students look at the stages in the *How to* box on the interactive whiteboard. Then they read the tapescript of recording 8.9 on page 156 and complete the gaps in the box in their books. Click on ⟨⟩ and ask a student to come to the interactive whiteboard to write on the lines to complete the *How to* box.

Click on ⟨⟩ to display the answers on the right.

> **ANSWERS:**
> Can bought doesn't exchange/like

b Students practise saying the dialogue to each other. Monitor closely, correcting any pronunciation errors.

TIP: *To review the stages of making a complaint, click on* ✐, *drag the slider to increase the width and using red (for example) ask a student to come to the interactive whiteboard and blank out all the stages. Then students can see if they can remember them. Click on* 🖊 *and erase the red to reveal the stages again. This can be done slowly to give students clues if they are having difficulty remembering. Alternatively, you could blank out the language on the right. If you blank out with one pen stroke, you can also click on* ⬉ *and drag the blank to reveal what was underneath.*

Close the flipchart by clicking X in the toolbar.
Return to the double spread by clicking on the zoomed-up area to make it smaller.
Click on the upwards pointing arrow ⬚ to return to Unit 8, and then ⬚ to return to the contents page to go to the next module.

⌐ Click on **page 85**. It will expand to fill the screen. Remember, you can zoom in to any part of the page by clicking on it, and return by clicking on it again.

Page 85

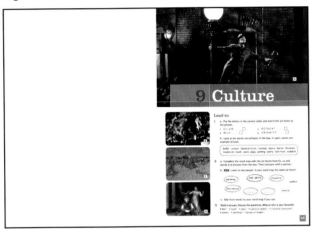

Flipchart: *Special flipchart p85*

Open the flipchart by clicking on the circled area and then on the Special Flipchart button ⚞.
Put the class into pairs and ask them to think of some ideas for each subject. Use the pen tool ✎ (in differing colours) to make some notes on the flipchart.
Close the flipchart by clicking X in the toolbar.

Flipchart: *Lead-in p85*

Open the flipchart by clicking on the circled area and then on Ⓐⓥ.
2a Students look at the picture of the incomplete word map. The head word is *The Arts*.

> **TIP:** *Make the spidergram more colourful and memorable by clicking on ✎ and highlighting the head word. Ask students which colour they would like. You can also change the background colour by clicking on 🎨 and choosing another colour.*

Explain there are five subheadings. Students use the words from Exercise 1a and 1b to complete the spidergram in their books. Tell students they can put words in more than one category if they wish. Students compare answers with a partner.
b Click on 🔊 to play recording 9.1. Students listen and compare their spidergram to that of the two people on the recording.
Click on ⌐ and ask a student to come to the interactive whiteboard to drag the words from the bottom to the correct group according to the listening.
Click on ⌐⌐⌐ to display the answers on a new page.
Click on 🔼 to return to 1 to compare your answers.

> **ANSWERS:**
> (This is the spidergram from the recording but there are several possible variations.) Painting: modern art;
> Literature: plays, poetry, novels;
> Music: dance, rock music, classical music, opera, ballet;
> Film: horror, comedy, cartoon;
> Theatre: plays, ballet, opera, dance

Click on ✎ and ask students to come to the interactive whiteboard to add any more words they can think of to the spidergram. (E.g. *architecture*, *modern dance*, etc.) You can do this on the Answers page if you wish.
Close the flipchart by clicking X in the toolbar.
Return to the page by clicking on the zoomed-up area to make it smaller.
Click on ▶ to go to the next double spread.

Double Spread p86/87

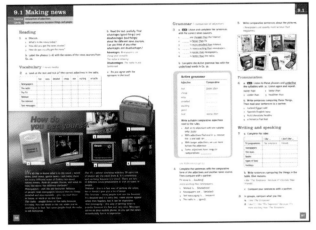

Flipchart: *Vocabulary p86*

Open the flipchart by clicking on the circled area and then on Ⓐⓥ.
2a Scanning. Explain to students that they will read the text in their books twice, the first time very quickly and the second time much more slowly. Click on ✎ and highlight and teach *detailed* (a lot of information) and *versatile* (you can do it in different ways and in different places). Direct students to the chart in their books. Tell students they have one minute to find the adjectives in the text and complete the chart. Stop the activity after a minute.
Click on ✎ and ask a student to come to the interactive whiteboard and write a tick in the white unshaded boxes to show the correct adjectives.
Click on 🧽 and check if there is a tick in the box by erasing the blue shading.

> **ANSWERS:**
> Newspapers: detailed / cheap / versatile
> The radio: easy
> The TV: exciting
> Teletext: fast
> The Internet: fast / detailed
> Text messages: fast / new

Close the flipchart by clicking X in the toolbar.
Return to the double spread by clicking on the zoomed-up area to make it smaller.

Flipchart: *Your Ideas* **p86**

Open the flipchart by clicking on the circled area and then on the Your Ideas button A⃞.

Ask students whether they watched/read the news today. What kind of news items did they see? In what way do they usually get the news? Make notes with the pen tool ✎.

Close the flipchart by clicking X in the toolbar.
Return to the double spread by clicking on the zoomed-up area to make it smaller.

Flipchart: *Grammar* **p87**

Open the flipchart by clicking on the circled area and then on A⃞V.
5 This exercise is on four pages, 1, 2, 3 and 4, with a pair of pictures on each page. Students identify the pairs of things in the pictures. Click on ✎ and annotate the pictures if necessary. Students then make sentences comparing the two in their books. An example is done for them. They can do this exercise in pairs. Click on ✎ and ask a student to come to the interactive whiteboard to write the comparison on the lines provided. Repeat for each page in turn by clicking on 2, 3, and 4. You can either check each page as you finish or finish the exercise and then click on 1 to return and start checking all the sentences together at the end.
Clicking on ⃞ will display possible answers below the lines.

> **SUGGESTED ANSWERS:**
> Newspapers are bigger than magazines. Modern books use larger pictures than classic ones. Black and white televisions are older than flat screen ones. New mobile phones are more expensive than old ones.

Close the flipchart by clicking X in the toolbar.
Return to the double spread by clicking on the zoomed-up area to make it smaller.

Flipchart: *Writing and speaking* **p87**

Open the flipchart by clicking on the circled area and then on A⃞V.
7a Students complete the table in their books by filling in examples of the names of things they like and don't like in the given categories. An example has been done for them. Click on ✎ and ask a student to come to the interactive whiteboard, choose a colour and write some examples.

> **TIP:** *If students would prefer to type their examples instead of writing, click on* T *in the toolbar to open the text tool, click where you want to type, go to the keyboard and type. You can select different fonts, change the size, colour and background etc.*

Other students can contribute and select different colours.
Click on 2
b Students can use the examples from Ex. 7a to give their reasons in Exercise b.
Close the flipchart by clicking X in the toolbar.
Return to the double spread by clicking on the zoomed-up area to make it smaller.
Click on ▷ to go to the next double spread.

Double Spread p88/89

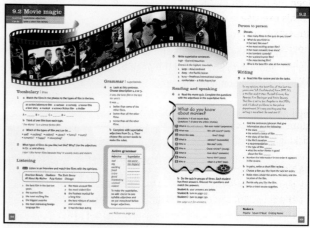

Flipchart: *Grammar* **p88**

Open the flipchart by clicking on the circled area and then on A⃞V.
4a Students look at the example sentence on the interactive whiteboard and then match it to the correct meaning. Students check answers in pairs. Click on ✐ and ask a student to come to the interactive whiteboard to highlight the correct choice.
Click on ⃞ to display a tick next to the correct answer.

> **ANSWER:**
> description 2

Click on 2.
b Students use the superlative adjectives from Ex. 3 to complete the Active grammar box in their books. The first two have been done for them. Students choose the correct option to complete the rules. Students check answers in pairs. Click on ✎ and ask a student to come to the interactive whiteboard to write the superlatives in the column on the right. Then click on ✐ and erase the incorrect words in the rules.
Click on ⃞ to highlight the correct words in the rules and display the superlatives on the right.

> **ANSWERS:**
> the most exciting, the freshest, the scariest, the best, the most interesting, the most unusual, the most violent
> Rules: *-est most*

Click on ✐ and use various colours to highlight the following points. Ask students: *What about two-syllable adjectives?* When they end in -y, we drop the -y and add *-iest*, e.g. *funny – funniest, scary – scariest*. For other two syllable adjectives we use the most, e.g. *famous – the most famous; polite – the most polite*.
Emphasise the use of the definite article in superlatives. (*'American Beauty' is best film* is incorrect.)
Use a different colour for ✐ and highlight the typical sentence stress used in superlative sentences. *It's the most <u>unusual</u> film.; It's the <u>freshest</u> <u>musical</u>*. Direct students to the Reference section on page 93.
Close the flipchart by clicking X in the toolbar.
Return to the double spread by clicking on the zoomed-up area to make it smaller.

Flipchart: *Reading and speaking* **p89**
Open the flipchart by clicking on the circled area and then on ⒜ⓥ.
6a This exercise is on ① and ②.
Students complete the questions in the quiz by inserting the superlative forms in their books. They check in pairs.
Click on ✎ and ask a student to come to the interactive whiteboard and write the superlatives on the lines provided to complete the questions. You can either check each page as you finish or click on ②, finish the exercise and then click on ① to return and check all together at the end.
Clicking on ▨▨▨ will display the answers below the lines.

> **ANSWERS:**
> 1 the most expensive 2 the earliest 3 the longest
> 4 the most successful 5 the richest 6 the youngest
> 7 the most romantic 8 the scariest 9 the worst

Close the flipchart by clicking X in the toolbar.
Return to the double spread by clicking on the zoomed-up area to make it smaller.
Click on ▸ to go to the next double spread.

Double Spread p90/91

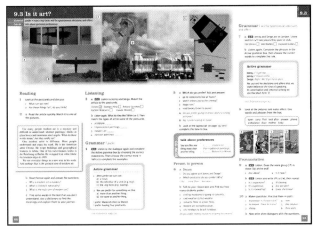

Flipchart: Your Ideas **p90**
Open the flipchart by clicking on the circled area and then on the Your Ideas button ⒜↑.
Ask students to look at the picture in their books or on the screen. Let them have small group discussions on the questions on the questions. Make notes on their suggestions using the pen tool ✎
Close the flipchart by clicking X in the toolbar.
Return to the double spread by clicking on the zoomed-up area to make it smaller.

Flipchart: *Listening* **p90**
Open the flipchart by clicking on the circled area and then on ⒜ⓥ.
3a Ask students: *Do you buy postcards or posters of your favourite paintings? Why?* Click on ▨ to play recording 9.5. Students listen and match the artists to the postcards in their books. The first one is done for them. Students check answers in pairs.
Click on ↖ and ask a student to come to the interactive whiteboard to drag the artist names from the bottom to the side of the postcard.
Click on ▨▨▨ to display the answers above or below the pictures.

> **ANSWERS:**
> A Damien Hirst B Antony Gormley C Claude Monet
> D Christo E Kazimir Malevich

Click on ②.
b Click on ▨ to play the recording a second time. Students listen and, in their books, write the name of the speaker beside the art they like. Students check answers in pairs. Click on ✎ and ask a student to come to the interactive whiteboard to write the initial letter of the speaker who likes that type of art on the lines.
Click on ▨▨▨ to display the answers under the lines.
Click on ③
Students match the types of art to the pictures. Students check answers in pairs. Click on ✎ and ask a student to come to the interactive whiteboard to write the letter of the postcard that represents that type of art in the boxes.
Click on ▨▨▨ to display the answer next to the boxes.

> **ANSWERS:**
> 1 S 2 S C 3 J 4 J
> 1 B 2 C 3 D 4 E

> **TIP:** *Click on* ① *and take a class vote on the most popular art in the class. Click on* ✎ *and write how many votes for each piece of art on the interactive whiteboard.*

Close the flipchart by clicking X in the toolbar.
Return to the double spread by clicking on the zoomed-up area to make it smaller.
Click on ▸ to go to the next double spread.

Double Spread p92/93

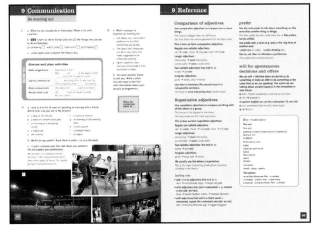

Flipchart: *Communication* **p92**
Open the flipchart by clicking on the circled area and then on ⒜ⓥ.
1b Teach *very crowded* (a lot of people there). Click on ▨ to play recording 9.9. Students listen and, in their books, tick the things the friends decide to do on Saturday. Students check answers in pairs.
Click on ✎ and ask a student to come to the interactive whiteboard to write a tick in the boxes next to the things that the friends decide to do on Saturday.
Click on ▨▨▨ to display the answers next to the boxes.

> **ANSWERS:**
> have lunch / go shopping

Click on ‹2› .

c Click on ◉ to play the recording again. Students listen and complete the *How to* box in their books. Students check answers in pairs. Click on ✎ and ask a student to come to the interactive whiteboard and write on the lines to complete the gaps.

Click on ▭ to display the answers in boxes on the right.

> **ANSWERS:**
> don't / go / Let's; prefer / than; more / We'll;

> **TIP:** *To review, click on* ✎ *and highlight the different ways of making suggestions and elicit the appropriate responses. (E.g. That sounds like fun and I prefer ... are both used in the tapescript.)*

Close the flipchart by clicking X in the toolbar.

Return to the double spread by clicking on the zoomed-up area to make it smaller.

Click on the upwards pointing arrow ▲ to return to Unit 9, and then on ▭ to return to the contents page to go to the next module.

Click on **page 95**. It will expand to fill the screen. Remember, you can zoom in to any part of the page by clicking on it, and return by clicking on it again.

Page 95

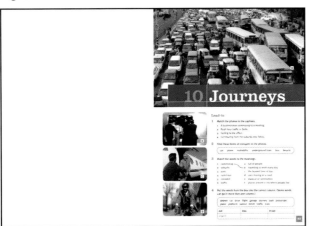

Flipchart: *Lead-in* **p95**

Open the flipchart by clicking on the circled area and then on [AV]. 3 Students match the words 1–6 to their meanings a–f in their books and check answers in pairs. The first one has been done for them. Click on ꖼ and ask a student to come to the interactive whiteboard to drag the meanings up and down until they match the words on the left.

Click on [   ] to display the answers on the right.

> **ANSWERS:**
> 1 commuting /b 2 suburbs /f 3 park /e 4 rush hour/c
> 5 crowded /a 6 traffic /d

Say the words and students note the word stress in each word. Focus on the /ʌ/ sound in s*u*burbs and r*u*sh hour.

> **TIP:** *Click on* ✏ *and ask students to identify the word stress in each word/phrase and then highlight it for them. Adjust the width of* ✏ *using the slider in the toolbar and you can place a 'blob' over the stressed syllable. Stress is underlined in the answers above.*

Click on [2].

In pairs, students look at the three headings in the table in their books. They put the words in the box into the correct columns. Some words can go into more than one column.

Click on ꖼ and ask a student to come to the interactive whiteboard to drag the words from the box into the correct column.

Click on [   ] to display the answers below the columns.

> **ANSWERS:**
> AIR: airport, flight, journey, passenger, plane, ticket
> RAIL: journey, passenger, platform, station, ticket, train
> ROAD: car, drive, garage, journey, park, passenger, traffic

> **TIP:** *Click on* ✏ *and highlight words that can go in more than one column. Use a different colour and highlight parts of speech. (nouns, verbs, both)*

Extend the Lead-in: Students work in groups of three or four. They choose four ways to improve the traffic situation in their local town/city or the city they are studying in. If traffic is not a problem students can focus on a city like Delhi or Tokyo. (E.g. more bus lanes, pay more to park in the city centre, etc.) Each group presents their 'solutions' to the rest of the class. Click on ➡ to go to a clean page and click on ✏ and write all the solutions on the interactive whiteboard and the class vote on what they consider to be the two most effective solutions. Don't worry about students making mistakes during this activity. Note down any obvious errors to deal with later.

Close the flipchart by clicking X in the toolbar.

Return to the page by clicking on the zoomed-up area to make it smaller.

Click on [»] to go to the next double spread.

Double Spread p96/97

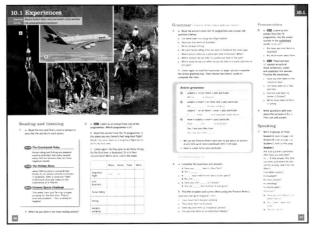

Flipchart: *Grammar* **p97**

Open the flipchart by clicking on the circled area and then on [AV]. 4a Students complete the questions and answers in their books using the Present Perfect. Students check answers in pairs. Click on ✏ and ask a student to come to the interactive whiteboard and write on the lines to fill in the gaps.

Click on [   ] to display the answers below the lines.

> **ANSWERS:**
> 1 ever, have 2 Has, hasn't 3 been, went

Click on [2].

b Students find and correct the mistakes in their books with a partner. Go through the example given in their books.

Click on ✒ and ask a student to come to the interactive whiteboard to erase the mistake if necessary. Click on ✏, ask students to choose an appropriate colour to correct and write in the correction.

TIP: *If students make a mistake, click on the Undo button ↺ in the toolbar to delete the last stroke. You can change the width of the eraser by moving the slider on the toolbar to make it narrower.*

You can either check each correction as you work through by clicking on individual [CHECK]s at the end of the lines or check all together at the end by clicking on [CHECK] at the bottom. Clicking on [CHECK] will display the answers in boxes below the sentences.

ANSWERS:
1 I have never been bungee jumping. 2 They have never been to Scotland. 3 Have you ever been to a classical concert? 4 Have you ever been on an adventure holiday?

Close the flipchart by clicking X in the toolbar.
Return to the double spread by clicking on the zoomed-up area to make it smaller.

Flipchart: *Pronunciation* p97
Open the flipchart by clicking on the circled area and then on [AV].
5a Click on ✎ and write *India* and *Greece* on the interactive whiteboard. Say the words and write the phonetic symbol /ɪ/ under *India* and the symbol /iː/ under *Greece*. Say the two sounds. Students look at the extract. Click on [🔊] on the left of 1 to play recording 10.2. Students listen and identify the sound of the underlined words. Students check answers in pairs. Click on ✎ and ask a student to come to the interactive whiteboard and write the sound in the boxes next to the question/answer.
Click on [CHECK] to display the answers next to the boxes.

ANSWER:
/ɪ/ /ɪ/

b Students look at the four sentences. First they predict where the four /ɪ/ sounds will be in each sentence with a partner. Click on [🔊] on the left of 5b to play recording 10.3. Students listen and identify the four /ɪ/ sounds in each sentence. Check in pairs. Click on ✎ and ask a student to come to the interactive whiteboard to highlight the sounds. Chose a colour – but not green.
Click on [CHECK] to highlight the answers in green.

ANSWERS:
1 Have you been to the cinema in Italy? 2 I've never been on a ship with him. 3 Has she ever been to dinner in Finland? 4 We've never been to Paris in spring.

Close the flipchart by clicking X in the toolbar.
Return to the double spread by clicking on the zoomed-up area to make it smaller.
Click on [▷] to go to the next double spread.

Double Spread p98/99

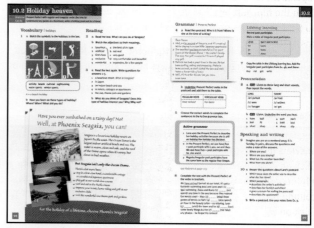

Flipchart: *Vocabulary* p98
Open the flipchart by clicking on the circled area and then on [AV].
1a Students look at the pictures of different types of holidays. Students match the words in the box to the pictures in their books. The first one has been done for them. Students check answers in pairs.
Click on ⤧ and ask a student to come to the interactive whiteboard to drag the words from the box next to the symbols they refer to.
Click on [CHECK] to display the answers above the symbols.

ANSWERS:
A beach B winter sports C activity D sightseeing
E water sports F cultural

TIP: *To review this vocabulary and practise spelling, click on ✎ , ask students to choose a colour, select a thick width by dragging the slider in the toolbar to the right, and ask a student to come to the interactive whiteboard and blank out all the vocabulary. Then they quiz students on the words. Click on 🧽 and as the students say and spell the words, the student at the interactive whiteboard can erase the colour and reveal the words. If students are having problems, erase slowly to give them clues.*

Close the flipchart by clicking X in the toolbar.
Return to the double spread by clicking on the zoomed-up area to make it smaller.

Flipchart: *Your Ideas* p98
Open the flipchart by clicking on the circled area and then on the Your Ideas button [AV].
Use this area to collate ideas from your students.
Talk about the students' favourite holiday experiences. Make notes with the pen tool ✎ .
Close the flipchart by clicking X in the toolbar.
Return to the double spread by clicking on the zoomed-up area to make it smaller.

Flipchart: *Grammar* **p99**

Open the flipchart by clicking on the circled area and then on AV̄ .
4b Students focus on the two underlined verb forms in the postcard in their books. Click on ✏ and underline them on the interactive whiteboard. Ask: *What tense is this?* (Present Perfect) *Which verb is regular?* (we've arrived, -ed ending) *Which is irregular?* (*has been*, no -*ed* ending) Direct students to the table in their books. Students read the postcard again and underline all the Present Perfect verbs. They decide whether the verbs are regular or irregular and add them to the table. Students check answers in pairs.

Click on ⤵ and ask a student to come to the interactive whiteboard to drag the verbs from the postcard into the correct column on the right.

Click on ▢ to display the answers on a new page.

Click on ⬆ to return to 1 to compare your answers.

> **ANSWERS:**
> REGULAR VERB: we've arrived, haven't played, she's visited
> IRREGULAR VERB: has been, I've spent, I've seen, has had, she's taken

> **TIP:** *For further practice, click on* 1 *to return to the finished exercise, click on* ▣ *and drag the cover to the right to reveal the postcard with gaps. Click on* ✏ *and ask a student to come to the interactive whiteboard and try to fill in all the missing words. Click on* ▣ *to remove the cover and click on* ▢ *to check the postcard again. Click on* ⬆ *to return to* 1 . *Alternatively, on* 1 , *click on* ⤵ *and drag the verbs back. You can also drag what you have written too.*

Close the flipchart by clicking X in the toolbar.
Return to the double spread by clicking on the zoomed-up area to make it smaller.

Flipchart: *Pronunciation* **p99**

Open the flipchart by clicking on the circled area and then on AV̄ .
8a Write *ship* and *sheep* on the interactive whiteboard. Say the two words and ask students *Which sound is longer?* (the /iː/ in *sheep*). Write the short /ɪ/ sound under *ship* and the long /iː/ sound under *sheep* and explain that /ː/ tells us that the sound is a long sound.
Students focus on the table. Click on ▢ on the left of the table to play recording 10.4. Students listen and repeat the words.

> **TIP:** *In the audio window, if you want to repeat a word, just drag the slider back and then release. If you want to pause to give students time to repeat, just click on the slider and hold it while students repeat and then release. Alternatively, click on pause and then play.*

b In pairs, students look at the six pairs of words and decide which word has a long vowel sound and which a short vowel sound. Click on ▢ to play recording 10.5. Students listen and circle the word they hear from each pair in their books. Students check answers in pairs. Click on ✏ and ask a student to come to the interactive whiteboard to highlight the word they heard.
Click on ▢ to highlight the answers.

> **ANSWERS:**
> 1 have 2 fit 3 short 4 park 5 bald 6 sleep

Close the flipchart by clicking X in the toolbar.
Return to the double spread by clicking on the zoomed-up area to make it smaller.
Click on ▣ to go to the next double spread.

Double Spread p100/101

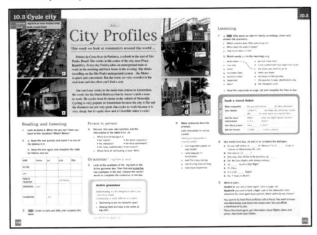

Flipchart: *Your Ideas* **p101**

Open the flipchart by clicking on the circled area and then on the Your Ideas button ◭.
Use the photos as prompts when discussing how students travel to/from work or school. Use the ✏ tool, and remember you can print out the class notes at any time.
Close the flipchart by clicking X in the toolbar.
Return to the double spread by clicking on the zoomed-up area to make it smaller.

Flipchart: *Special flipchart* **p100**

Open the flipchart by clicking on the circled area and then on the Special Flipchart button ◭.
Ask students to think about cities they have visited. Ask them to think about where the city is, what they saw there, what it is famous for etc. When they have finished making their own notes, ask them to come up to the interactive whiteboard and, using the ⤵ tool, drag the pin to where the city is located on the map. The class can then ask them questions about the city.
Close the flipchart by clicking X in the toolbar.

Flipchart: *Grammar* **p101**

Open the flipchart by clicking on the circled area and then on AV̄ .
6 Students use the prompts to make sentences in their books with the -ing form as the subject of the sentences. An example is done for them. Students check answers in pairs. Click on ⤵ and ask a student to come to the interactive whiteboard to drag the prompts onto the line provided leaving space to write. Click on ✏ (use a contrasting colour like red), and write the necessary changes and add words to make the complete sentence. This focuses students on the spelling changes, capital letters and verb form. You can either check each sentence as you work through by clicking on the small individual ▢ s or check all the sentences together at the end by clicking on the larger ▢ at the bottom.
Clicking on ▢ will display the answers below the lines.

ANSWERS:

1 Eating vegetables is good for your health. 2 Cycling is popular in Amsterdam. 3 Waiting for a bus is boring. 4 Living in a big city is exciting. 5 Taking taxis is expensive.

Close the flipchart by clicking X in the toolbar.
Return to the double spread by clicking on the zoomed-up area to make it smaller.

Flipchart: *Listening* **p101**

Open the flipchart by clicking on the circled area and then on AV .
7a Students look at the questions. Click on 🔊 to play recording 10.7. Students listen and answer the questions in their books. They check answers in pairs. Click on ✏ and ask a student to come to the interactive whiteboard to write the answers along the lines provided.
Click on ▭ to display the answers below the lines.

ANSWERS:

1 New Zealand 2 Friday the fifth of next month 3 Air New Zealand is six thousand NZ dollars (about 2000 pounds) or Qantas is 2300 pounds

Click on 2 .

b Students look at the vocabulary from the listening text and match the words to their meanings. The first one has been done for them. Click on ⬉ and ask a student to come to the interactive whiteboard to drag the meanings on the right up and down until they match the words on the left.
Click on ▭ to display the answers on the right.

ANSWERS:

1 destin̲ation. /c 2 one-way /f 3 ret̲urn /a 4 ec̲onomy class /g 5 b̲usiness class /b 6 dep̲arture /d 7 dir̲ect /e

> **TIP:** *Click on* ✏ *and ask students to identify the word stress in each word/phrase and then highlight it for them. Adjust the width of* ✏ *using the slider in the toolbar and you can place a 'blob' over the stressed syllable. Note: The stress falls on the second syllable in both direct and return. Destination and economy are both four-syllable words but the word stress is different in each. Stress is underlined in the answers above.*

Click on 3 .

c Teach *to book.* (to ask someone to keep something for you, e.g. a table in a restaurant, tickets to the theatre.) Students read the tapescript on page 158. Click on 🔊 to play the recording while they read. Students read and complete the *How to* box in their books and check answers in pairs.
Click on ✏ and ask a student to come to the interactive whiteboard to write the missing words on the lines.
Click on ▭ to display the answers on a new page.
Click on ⬆ to return to 3 to compare your answers.

ANSWERS:

tickets go want time direct much four

Students practise saying the sentences.
Click on ✏ to highlight the use of *would* in *I'd like to go/I'd like four tickets. I like four tickets* is incorrect in this context.

Close the flipchart by clicking X in the toolbar.
Return to the double spread by clicking on the zoomed-up area to make it smaller. Click on the upwards pointing arrow ⬆ to return to Unit 10, and then ⬅ to return to the contents page to go to the next module.

Click on **page 105**. It will expand to fill the screen. Remember, you can zoom in to any part of the page by clicking on it, and return by clicking on it again.

Page 105

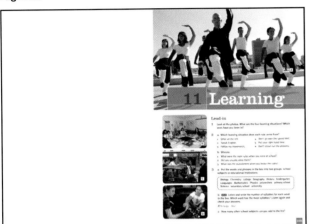

Flipchart: *Your Ideas* **p105**
Open the flipchart by clicking on the circled area and then on the Your Ideas button ⧉.
Use this area to collate ideas from your students.
Using the pen tool ✎ write down as many ideas as your class can think of. See if the students can think of any creative ideas for future learning.
Close the flipchart by clicking X in the toolbar.

Flipchart: *Lead-in* **p105**
Open the flipchart by clicking on the circled area and then on ⧉.
3a Students look at the words in the box in their books and put them into two groups: 'school subjects' and 'educational institutions'. Students can use their dictionaries for this activity. They compare answers in pairs. Click on ⦜ and ask a student to come to the interactive whiteboard to drag the vocabulary from the box at the top into the correct column. Click on ⬚ to display the answers under the two columns.

> **ANSWERS:**
> SCHOOL SUBJECTS: Biology, Chemistry, Geography, History, Languages, Mathematics, Physics, Science
> EDUCATIONAL INSTITUTIONS: college, kindergarten, polytechnic, primary school, secondary school, university

Click on ❷ .
b Students look at the vocabulary items again. In pairs they decide how many syllables each word has. Click on ⬤ to play recording 11.1. Students listen to check the number of syllables and then check their answers in pairs.
Click on ✎ and ask a student to come to the interactive whiteboard to write the number of syllables next to each word. Play the recording again as necessary for your students and repeat individual words.
Click on ⬚ to display the answers in boxes at the end of the lines.

> **ANSWERS:**
> Biology 4 Chemistry 3 college 2 Geography 3 History 2 kindergarten 4 Languages 3 Mathematics 4 Physics 2 polytechnic 4 primary school 4 Science 2 secondary school 4 university 5

> **TIP:** *Click on* ✎ *and use different colours to underline words with the same number of syllables. Click on* ✐ *, choose another colour and add a 'blob' over the stressed syllable. (Stress is underlined in the answers above.)*

Click on ❶ , click on ✎ and ask students if they can add any more examples to the list of school subjects. Count syllables and add stress as before.
Close the flipchart by clicking X in the toolbar.
Return to the page by clicking on the zoomed-up area to make it smaller.
Click on ⧉ to go to the next double spread.

Double Spread p106/107

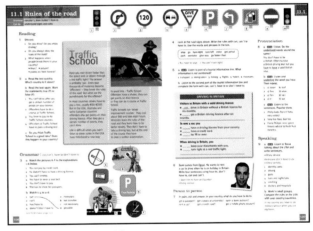

Flipchart: *Grammar* **p106**
Open the flipchart by clicking on the circled area and then on ⧉.
3a Students look at the pictures. Elicit where each picture is. (E.g. A on a train; B at an airport; C in a restaurant or shop; D, E, F – on a road.) Students match the six sentences to the pictures in their books. Check answers in pairs. Click on ⦜ and ask a student to come to the interactive whiteboard to drag the explanations onto the correct picture. (Try not to cover the letters on the pictures.) Click on ⬚ to display the answers to the right of each letter.

> **ANSWERS:**
> A 3 B 6 C 1 D 5 E 2 F 4

Click on ❷ .
b Students work in pairs and match the verbs to the meanings in their books. The first one has been done for them. Click on ✎ and ask a student to come to the interactive whiteboard to draw a line showing the matches.

TIP: *Click on* ✎ *to erase any mistakes or* ↺ *to undo the last stroke.*

Click on ⬚ to display the answers on the right.

ANSWERS:
1/d 2/b 3/a 4/c

Close the flipchart by clicking X in the toolbar.
Return to the double spread by clicking on the zoomed-up area to make it smaller.

Flipchart: *Grammar* **p107**
Open the flipchart by clicking on the circled area and then on ⬚.
5a Tell students they are going to listen to a computer operated telephone line giving tourist information. Students look at the list of options in their books. Click on 🔊 to play recording 11.2.

TIP: *Drag the audio window so that it is not covering any of the options.*

Students listen and identify which information is not mentioned. They check answers in pairs. Click on ✎ and ask a student to come to the interactive whiteboard and erase the information which was not mentioned.
Click on ⬚ to highlight the answers.

ANSWERS:
Flights and museums are not mentioned.

Click on 2 .
b This exercise is on 2 and 3 . Students look at the information box on driving in Britain. Teach *documents* (ID card, driving licence, etc.) and a *valid licence* (up to date). Click on 🔊 to play the second part of the recording. Students listen and complete the information box in their books. Students check answers in pairs.
Click on ✎ and ask a student to come to the interactive whiteboard to write on the lines to complete the information in the form. You can either check each page as you finish or click on 3 , finish the exercise and then click on 2 to return and check all the gaps together at the end.
Clicking on ⬚ will display the answers on the left.

ANSWERS:
can / have to; have to / have to / have to;
don't have to / can't

Close the flipchart by clicking X in the toolbar.
Return to the double spread by clicking on the zoomed-up area to make it smaller.

Flipchart: *Pronunciation* **p107**
Open the flipchart by clicking on the circled area and then on ⬚.
8a Students read the sentence. *Have* is underlined twice. Click on 🔊 to play recording 11.3. Students listen and decide if the pronunciation of *have* changes. Elicit students' answers, click on ✎ and write the answer on the lines provided. Click on ⬚ to display the answer below the line.

ANSWER:
No. The pronunciation of the ending of *have* is different in each case: /f/ and /v/.

Click on 2 .
b Students look at the pairs of words. Click on ✎ and write the phonetic symbols /f/ and /v/ on the interactive whiteboard.
Click on 🔊 for each pair of words in turn, to play recording 11.4. Students listen and identify which sound they hear in their books and check answers in pairs. For number 3, drag the audio window so that it is not covering those words.
Ask a student to come to the interactive whiteboard and click on each 🔊 in turn, to play the recording for one pair. Click on ✎ and highlight the word that is said. Repeat for each pair. Click on ⬚ to highlight the answers.

ANSWERS:
1 b 2 a 3 a 4 a

Click on 🔊 next to 8c to play recording 11.5. Students listen to the sentences and repeat. Then they practise saying them to a partner.
Close the flipchart by clicking X in the toolbar.
Return to the double spread by clicking on the zoomed-up area to make it smaller.
Click on ▶▶ to go to the next double spread.

Double Spread p108/109

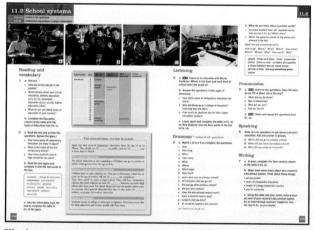

Flipchart: *Your Ideas* **p108**
Open the flipchart by clicking on the circled area and then on the Your Ideas button ⬚.
Use this area to collate ideas/stories/reminiscences about the students' school days.
Use the pen tool ✎ to make notes and the eraser tool ✎ if anyone makes any mistakes.
Close the flipchart by clicking X in the toolbar.
Return to the double spread by clicking on the zoomed-up area to make it smaller.

Flipchart: *Grammar* **p109**
Elicit as many question words as the students know. Start with the *wh-* question words from the previous exercise.
Open the flipchart by clicking on the circled area and then on ⬚.
4a Students look at the eight question words and match them to the correct ending in their books. Students check answers in pairs. Click on ⬚ and ask a student to come to the interactive

whiteboard to drag the question endings on the right up and down until they match the question words to form correct questions.

> **TIP:** *'Park' temporarily unwanted endings on top of the lines to avoid overwriting.*

Click on [image] to display the answers on the right.

> **ANSWERS:**
> 1/e 2/h 3/d 4/a 5/g 6/c 7/b 8/f

> **TIP:** *For further practice, click on [image], drag the cover to the left to cover the question words and see if students can remember the question words.*

Direct students to the reference section on page 113.
Close the flipchart by clicking X in the toolbar.
Return to the double spread by clicking on the zoomed-up area to make it smaller.
Click on [image] to go to the next double spread.

Double Spread p110/111

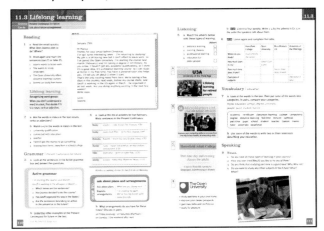

Flipchart: *Grammar* **p110**
Open the flipchart by clicking on the circled area and then on [image].
4a This exercise is on [1] and [2].

Click on [image] and highlight *flatmate*. Check the meaning with the students: (people you live with, not your family). Direct students to the calendar extract in their books. Ask: *How many flatmates are there? What are their names?* (4: Kimiko, Jesus, Pilar, Radek) Ask: *Are these suggestions or definite arrangements which the four people have made?* (Definite arrangements, times and places are decided on.)
Students look at the example and write the sentences in their books using the Present Continuous. Students check answers in pairs. Click on [image] and ask a student to come to the interactive whiteboard to write the sentences along the lines provided. (Try not to write too large, to avoid overlapping with the answers.) You can either check each page as you finish or click on [2], finish the writing and then click on [1] to return and check all the sentences together at the end.
Clicking on [image] will display the answers below the lines.

> **ANSWERS:**
> Juan and Pilar are going to the cinema at quarter to nine on Tuesday. Radek is starting his new English class at half past six on Wednesday.
> Juan is meeting his brother at the Italian restaurant at eight o'clock on Thursday. Everyone is going to a nightclub at half past ten on Friday. Kimiko is taking a flight to Tokyo at ten to twelve on Saturday.

Direct students to the *How to* box in their books.
Close the flipchart by clicking X in the toolbar.
Return to the double spread by clicking on the zoomed-up area to make it smaller.

Flipchart: *Listening* **p111**
Open the flipchart by clicking on the circled area and then on [image].
6 Click on [image] to play the recording 11.10 again. Students listen and complete the table in their books. Students check answers in pairs.
Click on [image] and ask a student to come to the interactive whiteboard to write in each column to complete the table.
Click on [image] to display the answers on a new page.
Click on [image] to return to [1] to compare your answers.

> **ANSWERS:**
> Haresfield College: / £100 a year / 3 hours a week / History, Languages, Computing.
> Open University: at home / / 12 hours a week / doesn't say.
> MicroMatters Ltd: the centre / £900 / / computer skills.
> University of the Third Age: halls or schools all over the country / £2.50 to join / doesn't say /

Close the flipchart by clicking X in the toolbar.
Return to the double spread by clicking on the zoomed-up area to make it smaller.
Click on [image] to go to the next double spread.

Double Spread p112/113

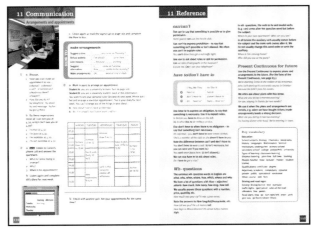

Flipchart: *Communication* **p112**
Open the flipchart by clicking on the circled area and then on [image].
2a Students read the questions. Click on [image] to play recording 11.11. Students listen and answer the questions in their books. Students check answers. Click on [image] and ask a student to come to the interactive whiteboard to write along the lines provided.
Click on [image] in the middle of the page on the right to display the answers for 2a below the lines.

ANSWERS:

1 an appointment with his son's teacher 2 to talk about his examinations 3 Tuesday morning at 9 o'clock

b Click on [icon] to play the recording again. Students listen and complete Jill's diary in their books. Students check answers in pairs. Click on / and ask a student to come to the interactive whiteboard to write and complete the diary.
Click on [icon] to display the answers on the right.

ANSWERS:

Tuesday teaching / swimming; Wednesday teaching / teaching; Thursday teaching / free

Close the flipchart by clicking X in the toolbar.
Return to the double spread by clicking on the zoomed-up area to make it smaller.

Flipchart: *Special flipchart* **P112**
Open the flipchart by clicking on the circled area and then on the Special Flipchart button [icon].
This speaking practice can be used with students in A/B pairs.
Use the eraser tool [icon] to remove the top row of the table, revealing the first scenario for students to role-play. Ask the students to imagine themselves in this situation and then to swap roles.
Close the flipchart by clicking X in the toolbar.
Return to the double spread by clicking on the zoomed-up area to make it smaller.
Click on the upwards pointing arrow [icon] to return to Unit 11, and then [icon] to return to the contents page to go to the next module.

Click on **page 115**. It will expand to fill the screen. Remember, you can zoom in to any part of the page by clicking on it, and return by clicking on it again.

Page 115

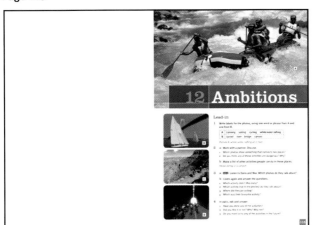

Flipchart: *Your Ideas* **p115**

Open the flipchart by clicking on the circled area and then on the Your Ideas button .

Use this area to collate ideas from your students.

Talk about the students' adventure activity experiences. Make notes with the pen tool .

Close the flipchart by clicking X in the toolbar.

Return to the double spread by clicking on the zoomed-up area to make it smaller.

Flipchart: *Lead-in* **p115**

Open the flipchart by clicking on the circled area and then on .

1 This exercise is on two pages 1 and 2 , with two pictures on each page. Students look at the four photos of various adventure sports. They choose one word or phrase from box A and from box B to match each of the pictures in their books. Students check answers in pairs. Picture A is done as an example in their books.

Click on and ask a student to come to the interactive whiteboard and write a label on the lines next to each picture. Tell students they will have to add a preposition and an article. You can either check each page as you finish or click on 2 , finish the exercise and then click on 1 to return and check all together at the end. Clicking on will display the answers below the lines.

> **ANSWERS:**
> A white water rafting on a river B sailing under a bridge
> C trekking in a canyon D cycling through a tunnel

Close the flipchart by clicking X in the toolbar.

Return to the page by clicking on the zoomed-up area to make it smaller.

Click on to go to the next double spread.

Double Spread p116/117

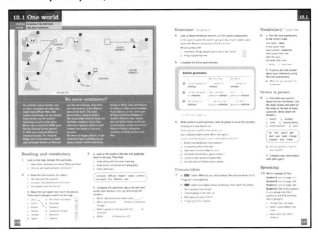

Flipchart: *Reading and vocabulary* **p116**

Open the flipchart by clicking on the circled area and then on .

3b Students complete the questions with the words and write the answers in their books. Students check in pairs. Click on and ask a student to come to the interactive whiteboard to drag the correct words from the box at the top to complete the questions.

Click on and write the answers along the lines provided.

Click on to display the answers at the ends of the questions and below the lines.

> **ANSWERS:**
> 1 difficult / rivers, mountains and seas 2 connect / 1994
> 3 island / a tunnel 4 continent / Asia

Close the flipchart by clicking X in the toolbar.

Return to the double spread by clicking on the zoomed-up area to make it smaller.

Flipchart: *Vocabulary* **p117**

Open the flipchart by clicking on the circled area and then on .

8a Students look at the future time expressions and put them in order starting from the nearest in time from now. The first two are done for them in their books. Students check answers in pairs.

Click on and ask a student to come to the interactive whiteboard to drag the expressions from the left into the correct order in the column on the right.

Click on to display the answers on the right.

> **ANSWERS:**
> 1 today 2 tomorrow 3 next week 4 the week after next 5 later this year 6 next summer 7 in two year's time
> 8 three years from now

Close the flipchart by clicking X in the toolbar.

Return to the double spread by clicking on the zoomed-up area to make it smaller.

Flipchart: *Special flipchart* **p117**

Ask students to talk in pairs about their plans for the future. At this stage, the plans can be about anything and with any timeframe.

Now open the flipchart by clicking on the circled area and then on the Special Flipchart button .

Each student can then come to the whiteboard and, using the 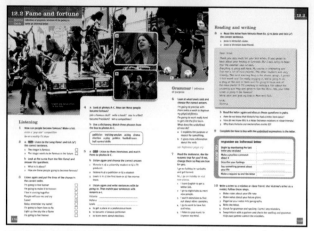k tool, choose one topic from the left side of the page and drag it into the box. They can then use the words in the smaller box above to help them talk about their plans in this area (these words are also draggable).

Close the flipchart by clicking X in the toolbar.

Return to the double spread by clicking on the zoomed-up area to make it smaller.

Click on ▷ to go to the next double spread.

Double Spread p118/119

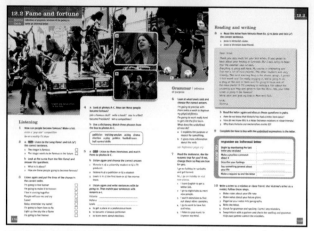

Flipchart: *Your Ideas* p118

Open the flipchart by clicking on the circled area and then on the Your Ideas button 🗛.

Use this area as a brainstorming page to encourage discussion about celebrity and famous historical/modern figures. Use the ✏ tool to make notes.

Close the flipchart by clicking X in the toolbar.

Return to the double spread by clicking on the zoomed-up area to make it smaller.

Flipchart: *Listening* p118

Open the flipchart by clicking on the circled area and then on 🗛.

3 Students look at the lines of the song chorus. Students listen and put the lines of the chorus into the correct order in their books. Students check answers in pairs. Click on k and ask a student to come to the interactive whiteboard to drag the lines up and down until they are in the correct order.

Click on ▭ to display the answers on a new page.

Click on ⌃ to return to ▭1 to compare your answers.

> **ANSWERS:**
> 1 Fame! 2 I'm going to live forever 3 I'm going to learn how to fly 4 I feel it coming together 5 People will see me and cry 6 I'm going to make it to heaven 7 Light up the sky like a flame 8 I'm going to live forever 9 Baby, remember my name!

> **TIP:** *Ask students if they would enjoy singing the song. Play it again and students can join in with the chorus on the interactive whiteboard.*

Close the flipchart by clicking X in the toolbar.

Return to the double spread by clicking on the zoomed-up area to make it smaller.

Flipchart: *Listening* p118

Open the flipchart by clicking on the circled area and then on 🗛.

5a Click on 🔘 next to each 'Interview' to play each part of recording 12.5. Students listen and match the speakers to the photos in their books. Students check answers in pairs. Click on k and ask students to say which interview goes with which picture. Drag the interview label under the correct picture.

Click on ▭ to display the answers below the lines.

> **ANSWERS:**
> A 2; B 1; C 3

Click on ▭2 .

b Students look at the sentences. Teach *reserve team* (not the first team). Click on 🔘 to play the recording again. Students listen and choose the answer. Students check in pairs. Click on ✒ and ask a student to come to the interactive whiteboard to erase the incorrect choice.

Click on ▭ on the right at the top to highlight the answers.

> **ANSWERS:**
> 1 a 2 b 3 b

c Students read the tapescript on page 160. Play the recording as they read. Students write sentences about what each speaker is going to do. Students look at the reasons a–c and match them to the sentences in their books. Students check in pairs. Click on ✏ and ask a student to come to the interactive whiteboard and write the sentences along the lines provided. Then write the letters in the boxes to show the correct reason.

Click on ▭ to display the answers below the lines and next to the boxes.

> **ANSWERS:**
> Victoria is going to learn how to sing and dance – b
> Helena is going to work for a politician next summer – c
> Lewis is going to practise with the reserve team twice a week – a

Close the flipchart by clicking X in the toolbar.

Return to the double spread by clicking on the zoomed-up area to make it smaller.

Click on ▷ to go to the next double spread.

Double Spread p120/121

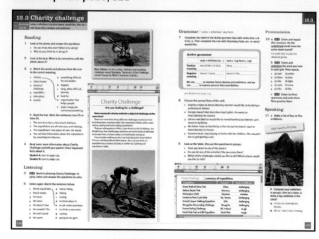

Flipchart: *Reading* **p120**

Open the flipchart by clicking on the circled area and then on A∨ .
3a Students focus on new vocabulary in the text. They look at the
words and match them to the definitions in their books. The first
one has been done for them. Students check answers in pairs.
Click on ⬉ and ask a student to come to the interactive
whiteboard to drag the meanings on the right up and down until
they correspond to the words on the left.
Click on ✔✔✔ to display the answers on the right.

ANSWERS:
2/f 3/a 4/c 5/b 6/d

> **TIP:** *Click on* ▣ *, drag the cover to the left to hide the words
> and see if students can remember them from the meanings.
> Alternatively, click on* ✐ *and blank out the words and check
> students' spelling as well. Click on* ⬤ *and erase slowly to give
> clues if students are having problems.*

Close the flipchart by clicking X in the toolbar.
Return to the double spread by clicking on the zoomed-up area to
make it smaller.

Flipchart: *Grammar* **p121**

Open the flipchart by clicking on the circled area and then on A∨ .
8 Students choose the correct form of the verb to complete the
sentences in their books. Students check in pairs. Click on ⬤ and
ask a student to come to the interactive whiteboard to erase the
incorrect choice.

> **TIP:** *If students make a mistake, click on the Undo button* ↺
> *to delete the last pen stroke.*

You can either click on ✔✔✔ at the end of each line to check
answers consecutively, or click on ✔✔✔ at the bottom to check
all the answers together.
Clicking on ✔✔✔ will highlight the answers.

ANSWERS:
1 dancing, to be 2 learning, to leave 3 to travel, flying
4 living, to leave 5 staying, to get

Close the flipchart by clicking X in the toolbar.
Return to the double spread by clicking on the zoomed-up area to
make it smaller.
Click on ▶ to go to the next double spread.

Double Spread p122/123

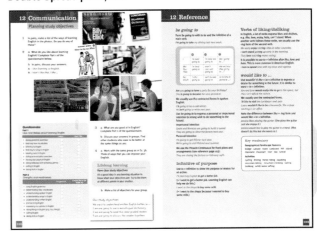

Flipchart: *Communication* **p122**

Open the flipchart by clicking on the circled area and then on A∨ .
1 Students look at the photos. In pairs, they use the pictures to
make a list of ways of learning English. Students discuss and add
to the list with ideas of their own. Click on ✐ and ask a student
to come to the interactive whiteboard to write their list.
Click on ✔✔✔ to display the answers on a new page.
Click on ◸ to return to 1 to compare your answers.

ANSWERS:
Read English newspapers; watch a film in English; listen
to English/American music; use a monolingual dictionary;
read graded readers; listen to tapes/CDs of English; look
at websites in English.

Discuss any additional ways students have mentioned. Click on
✐ and highlight any favourite methods.
Close the flipchart by clicking X in the toolbar.
Return to the double spread by clicking on the zoomed-up area to
make it smaller.
Click on the upwards pointing arrow ◸ to return to Unit 12, and
then ▯▯ to return to the contents page to go to the next module.

Film Bank

Film Bank flipchart – Meeting people
Go to the Film Bank area 🎬 Choose Unit 1. Open the flipchart by clicking on the flipchart bar.
1 Discuss the questions given on the flipchart. There are no correct answers given here, so encourage creativity. For part 3 of the exercise, divide the class up into A students and B students and ask them to pretend to be the characters in the photos.
Click on 2 to move to the next exercise.
2 After watching the film, use the pen tool ✏ to write in the correct extract number next to the names.
To reveal the answers click on the check button at the bottom.

> **ANSWERS:**
> a 4 b 6 c 1 and 7 d 7 e 2 f 5 g 3 and 5

Click on 3
3 Ask students to watch the film again and pay close attention to the welcoming phrases the people use. Use the pen tool ✏ to fill in the chart with students' suggestions.
To show the correct answers click on the check button at the bottom.

> **ANSWERS:**
> Good morning (1, 6) Good afternoon (4) Good evening (3, 5, 7) How do you do? (2, 7) May I introduce…? (7)

Close the flipchart by clicking X in the toolbar.

Film bank flipchart – Unreal city
Go to the Film Bank area 🎬 Choose Unit 2. Open the flipchart by clicking on the flipchart bar.
1 This flipchart ask students to use their dictionaries to check some of the more difficult vocabulary from the film. Put them into small groups or pairs and ask them to look at words 1–6 in their dictionaries. When they have decided which word goes with which picture, ask a volunteer to come up to the whiteboard and ⬉ to drag the appropriate word into the correct space.
To reveal the answers click on the check button at the bottom.

> **ANSWERS:**
> 1 B 2 C 3 F 4 A 5 D 6 E

Click on 2 to move to page 2.
Before watching the film 'Unreal City' ask the students to guess the correct order of the things that happen (a–j). The cartoon itself will clarify the positions of the letter, so avoid clicking the check button before you have shown the cartoon.

Use the pen tool ✏ to write the numbers into the box. Different students could use different colours to show varying opinions.

> **ANSWERS:**
> Correct order: b, e, d, i, h, c, a, f, g, j

Close the flipchart by clicking X in the toolbar.

Film bank flipchart – Deborah's day
Go to the Film Bank area 🎬 Choose Unit 3. Open the flipchart by clicking on the flipchart bar.
1 Discuss the questions given on the flipchart. There are no correct answers given here, so encourage creativity. Do students recognise any of the people in the photos?
Click on 2 to go to page 2.
2 Ask students to fill in the blanks in the sentences by using the arrow tool ⬉ to drag the words and phrases from the box.
To reveal the answers click on the check button and the answers will appear underneath the blanks.

> **ANSWERS:**
> 1 play 2 theatres 3 lines 4 personal stereo

Click on 3 to go to page 3.
3 Before watching the video, ask students to work in pairs and decide what they think actors do every day. Using the pen tool ✏ ask them to tick the boxes in the 'your ideas' columns.
Then watch 'Deborah's day'
4 Now ask students to tick the column labelled 'Deborah' and choose the appropriate activities.

> **ANSWERS:**
> get up early, do yoga, check emails and diary, send text messages, run in the park, practise her lines

Close the flipchart by clicking X in the toolbar.

Film bank flipchart – Two soups
Go to the Film Bank area 🎬 Choose Unit 4. Open the flipchart by clicking on the flipchart bar.
2 In their books, students match the expressions and explanations and check in pairs.
Click on ⬉ and ask a student to come to the interactive whiteboard and drag the phrases up or down in the column on the right to match the meanings.
To check your answers, click on at the bottom.

> **ANSWERS:**
> 1 c 2 e 3 a 4 b 5 d

Click on 2 to move to page 2
3 Use the top half of the flipchart to make notes on what goes wrong in the restaurant in the video. You can check the answer by clicking on the small button.

> **ANSWER:**
> The waitress is very slow and keeps forgetting things so the customers have to repeat their order. Unfortunately because she is deaf she has to keep walking back to the table to hear the customers which means everything takes even longer. When she eventually brings over their soup she manages to spills it all so the bowls are empty when she puts them on the table.

Click on 3 to move to the next exercise.
4 Students answer the questions about the film using the pen tool ✏

To check the answers click on the [　　] button at the bottom of the page. The answers will display below the lines.

ANSWERS:
1 twenty-five to 2 four (three customers and the waitress)
3 twice 4 four times 5 nothing

Close the flipchart by clicking X in the toolbar.

Film bank flipchart – ResidenSea
Go to the Film Bank area [　] Choose Unit 5. Open the flipchart by clicking on the flipchart bar.
1 Put the students into groups and ask them to talk about the pictures of the boats a, b and c and make notes on what your students may or may not know about them.
Then, ask students to think about the second question and ask a volunteer to explain their answer to the class.
Click on [2] to move to the next exercise.
2 In their books, students match the places and definitions and check in pairs.
Click on [↖] and ask a student to come to the interactive whiteboard and drag the phrases up or down in the column on the right to match the meanings.
To check the answers click on the [　　] button at the bottom of the page. The answers will display to the right of the box.

ANSWERS:
1 c 2 d 3 a 4 b

Click on [3]
3 Using the pen tool [✎] write T (true) or F (false) next to the statements. Then show the film to the class and see if they agree with their initial suggestions.
Use the [　　] button to ensure that the answers are correct.

ANSWERS:
1 T 2 F It hasn't got cars, offices or any of the stresses of modern life. 3 F Some people go for a holiday 4 F They aren't cheap (a three-bedroom apartment costs just over four million US dollars) 5 T 6 T

Close the flipchart by clicking X in the toolbar.

Film bank flipchart – Amazing buildings
Go to the Film Bank area [　] Choose Unit 6. Open the flipchart by clicking on the flipchart bar.
1 Ask students to look at the photos of the cities, either in their books or on screen. Using the [↖] tool, drag the photos left or right to match them with the appropriate city above.

ANSWERS:
London C, New York A, Sydney E, Paris B, Bilbao D

Use questions 2, 3 and 4 to discuss the topic further.
Click on [2] to move to the second page.
2 Ask the students to look at the photos more closely. Put the class into five groups, asking each group to try and identify the words/phrases from the flipchart in each photo.
Allow one member of each group to come up to the interactive whiteboard and use [↖] to drag the labels under the correct photo. If it is not clear which part of the photos are being referred to, use the pen tool [✎] to make it clearer.

To check the answers click on the [　　] button at the bottom of the page. The answers will display below the lines.

Click on [3] .
3 Go through the facts and figures in the chart as a class. Then watch the film. Using the pen tool [✎] tick the answers in the correct columns.
Click on [4] to continue the exercise.
Click on the [　　] button to see the answers on a separate page.

ANSWERS:

	The Flatiron Building	The Guggenheim Museum	The Eiffel Tower	The Gherkin	The Sydney Opera House
1 It opened in 1889.			✔		
2 It has 19 galleries.		✔			
3 It opened over 30 years ago.					✔
4 It's made of stone and metal.		✔			
5 It's only two metres wide.	✔				
6 It opened in 2004				✔	
7 It's 300 metres high.			✔		
8 Its roof comes from Sweden.					✔
9 It's 87 metres high.	✔				
10 The architect was Danish					✔

Close the flipchart by clicking X in the toolbar.
Film bank flipchart –Great Expectations
Go to the Film Bank area [　] Choose Unit 7. Open the flipchart by clicking on the flipchart bar.
1 Give the students some time to look at the pictures of the films in the photos. Use the space on the flipchart to make notes on any ideas the students have.
Click on [2] to move to the next exercise.
2 Ask students to read the sentences silently. Using the [↖] drag the correct word or phrase into place in the sentences.
Click on [　　] to check answers. The answers are displayed below each line.

ANSWERS:
1 novel 2 wedding dress 3 scared 4 scary 5 broken
6 Come along

Click on [3]

3 Watch the film and ask students to think about the most appropriate adjectives to describe the characters. Use the pen tool ✎ to tick the correct boxes.

ANSWERS:
The boy (Pip): scared, shy, thin, young. The girl (Estella): pretty, strange, young. The woman (Miss Havisham): old, rich, scary, strange, thin. The house: dark, large, old, scary, strange.

Close the flipchart by clicking X in the toolbar.

Film bank flipchart – The Notting Hill
Go to the Film Bank area ▦ Choose Unit 8. Open the flipchart by clicking on the flipchart bar.

1 and 2 Use this page to get some idea about what your class knows about carnivals and celebrations before you watch the film. Use the pen tool ✎ to make notes.

Click on [2] to move to the next page.

3 Ask students to read the text in their books quietly. Then watch the video.

The text on the screen is fully eraseable. Use the ✐ tool, to rub out the incorrect sections of text and write in the correct answers using the pen tool ✎.

Click on [____] to see the correct answers on a separate page.

ANSWERS:
The Notting Hill Carnival is a huge London carnival – about a **million** people come to be in the carnival or to watch it. It happens every **August**. There are about **70** bands with their own music, costumes and carnival queen. The costumes are very important for the carnival. Clary Salandy started designing costumes **15** years ago. Her carnival queen is a young woman called Tamiko, who **has had lots** of experience. She puts on her carnival costume – it's very **comfortable** because it's **not as heavy as it looks**. When it comes to the carnival weekend, the bands parade through the streets – the costumes look amazing and it's an **unforgettable** experience.

Close the flipchart by clicking X in the toolbar.

Film Bank flipchart – Spirit of the city
Go to the Film Bank area ▦ Choose Unit 9. Open the flipchart by clicking on the flipchart bar.

1 Use the painting by Richard Tate to prompt a discussion about London buildings. It is also useful when talking about art preferences.

There are no correct answers here, so encourage discussion rather than accuracy.

Click on [2]

2 This exercise helps to prepare students for the film. Ask if anyone recognises or knows the names of the buildings pictured. Make notes using the pen tool ✎.

ANSWERS:
A St Paul's Cathedral B Battersea Power Station C Tower Bridge D The Dome E The London Eye

Click on [3]

3 After watching the film, allow students to write on the whiteboard, using the pen tool ✎ to tick the correct box(es) for each building.

Close the flipchart by clicking X in the toolbar.

Film bank flipchart – Commuting
Go to the Film Bank area ▦ Choose Unit 10. Open the flipchart by clicking on the flipchart bar.

1 Use this flipchart page to discuss the questions. Put the class into small groups to discuss questions 1–3 and use the pen tool ✎ to make notes on their feedback.

Click on [2] to move to exercise 2.

2 In their books, students match the words and their meanings and check in pairs.

Click on ⇗ and ask a student to come to the interactive whiteboard and drag the phrases up or down in the column on the right to match the meanings.

To check the answers click on the [____] at the bottom display on the right side of the page.

ANSWERS:
1 e 2 c 3 g 4 h 5 a 6 b 7 d 8 f

Close the flipchart by clicking X in the toolbar.

Film Bank flipchart – Rock climbing
Go to the Film Bank area ▦ Choose Unit 11. Open the flipchart by clicking on the flipchart bar.

1 Use this area to make notes on students' own experiences.

Click on [2] to move to the second page and the second exercise

2 Click on ⇗ and ask a student to come to the interactive whiteboard and drag the meanings up or down in the column on the right to match the meanings.

To check your answers, click on the [____] at the bottom to display them on the right side of the page

ANSWERS:
1 c 2 f 3 b 4 a 5 d 6 e

Click on [3]

3 Check the vocabulary knowledge of your class. Use the ⇗ tool to drag the labels in the box to the correct pictures. Then watch the film to check if they are correct.

You can also check if the answers are correct by clicking on [____] at the bottom of the page.

ANSWERS:
A 4 B 3 C 2 D 1 E 5

Close the flipchart by clicking X in the toolbar.

Film bank flipchart – Ten great adventures
Go to the Film Bank area ▦ Choose Unit 12. Open the flipchart by clicking on the flipchart bar.

1 Use this flipchart page to discuss the questions. Put the class into small groups to discuss questions 1–3 and use the pen tool ✎ to make notes on their feedback.

Click on [2] to move to exercise 2.

2 Because of length, this exercise is on two pages [2] and [3]. In small groups ask the students to look at the photos and think of

labels for them. Ask members of each group to come up to the interactive whiteboard to write in their answers using the pen tool ✏.

Click on the ▭ to display the answers below the lines.

> **ANSWERS:**
> 1 diving 2 dog sledging 3 swimming with dolphins
> 4 parascending 5 whale watching 6 riding the rapids

Close the flipchart by clicking X in the toolbar.

Pearson Education Limited
Edinburgh Gate
Harlow
Essex, CM20 2JE
England
and Associated Companies throughout the world

www.longman.com

Activstudio was created and is licenced by Promethean. The publishers would like to thank Promethean and Activlingua for their invaluable help.

First published 2007

ISBN: 978-1-4058-9187-5

Printed in the UK by Ashford Colour Press Ltd

Set in Meta LF, 8.5pt

Publishing Management and Design by Starfish Design Editorial and Project Management Ltd.
Introduction adapted from material supplied by Sarah Walker.

All page reproduction material is taken from *Total English Elementary Students' Book*.
Written by Mark Foley and Diane Hall.
ISBN: 978-0-582-84177-2
© Pearson Education Limited 2005